Computers in the Primary School

Computers in the Primary School

Edited by
Ton Griffin
Leslie Bash

CASSELL

Cassell
Wellington House
125 Strand
London WC2R 0BB

215 Park Avenue South
New York
NY 10003

British Library Cataloguing-in-Publication Data
A catalogue record for this book is available from the British Library.

Library of Congress Cataloging-in-Publication Data
Computers in the primary school / edited by Jon Griffin and Leslie
  Bash.
     p.   cm. — (Cassell education)
  Includes index.
    ISBN 0–304–32997–5 : $70.00. — ISBN 0–304–32991–6 (pbk.) : $26.00
    1. Computer-assisted instruction. 2. Education, Elementary—Data
processing. 3. Educational technology. I. Griffin, Jon.
  II. Bash, Leslie. III. Series.
  LB1028.5.C57463 1995
  371.3'34—dc20   94–45160
                                                    CIP

ISBN 0–304–32997–5 (hardback)
     0–304–32991–6 (paperback)

Acknowledgements
John Lodge, 'With the eyes of a child', 1969 (p. 4), published by MCA Music Limited. Reprinted by permission of the publisher.
Justin Hayward, 'I never thought I'd live to be a hundred', 1969 (p. 61), published by Tyler Music Limited. Reprinted by permission of the publisher.
Extracts from Department of Education and Science Publications (pp. 25–8). Crown copyright is reproduced with the permission of the Controller of HMSO.

Typeset by York House Typographic Ltd
Printed and bound in Great Britain by Redwood Books, Trowbridge, Wiltshire

Contents

Notes on the Contributors

Leslie Bash is currently Principal Lecturer and Co-ordinator of Research in the Department of Education at Anglia Polytechnic University. He has specific interests in urban, multicultural and policy issues in education and has co-authored a number of books, including: *Urban Schooling* (1985); *The Education Reform Act: Competition and Control* (1989); and *Conflict and Contradiction: The 1988 Education Act in Action* (1991). He has also edited a collection of papers, *Comparative Urban Education* (1987), and is co-editor of the 1995 *World Yearbook of Education*.

Jon Griffin is a Principal Lecturer within Anglia Polytechnic University's Education Department and is Head of Curriculum Subjects, a team which includes the history, information technology, modern foreign languages, music, physical education, religious education, and technology subject areas. His interests include the use of new technologies and delivery systems in teacher education, control technology, multimedia, and course development. He was involved in the Computers in Jordan Project and has written a number of articles and presented papers at conferences in the USA.

Contributions to this book: co-editor; Chapter 1, 'Introduction'; Chapter 6, 'Learning Discovery Systems in the Computerized Classroom'; Chapter 7, 'Issues of Multimedia in the Learning Environment'; Chapter 9, 'Curriculum Developments'.

Kara Hales studied languages (French and German) at Epping Forest College in Loughton, Essex. Having completed her A levels, she took a year away from her studies before embarking upon her chosen career of primary teaching. Kara is currently a student at Anglia Polytechnic University, at Brentwood in Essex. She is following a Modular Primary Bachelor of Education degree course and specializing in English and Technology.

Stephen Heppell is based at Anglia Polytechnic University's UltraLab, which researches into learning where it is supported by computer and information techno logy. The UltraLab is located within the Department of Education. Current develop ment partners include the BBC, the British Film Institute, the Engineering Council Apple Computer (Europe), Essex Water and NASA.

Stephen has long experience of educational computing; he was originally with the United Kingdom government's Microelectronics Education Programme (MEP) and has been based at Anglia Polytechnic University (including its various previous forms since 1984. He has recently retired as chair of the Information Technology in Teacher Education group with an institutional membership of all the teacher training colleges in the UK. He is active on a number of UK government advisory groups and is chair of the Courseware Trust, a software charity for schools and teachers in Scotland and Northern Ireland.

Andy Lambert is the General Inspector for Information Technology for the London Borough of Haringey, where he monitors and reviews information technology in the National (and wider) Curriculum. Andy was originally a science teacher, doing research into problem-solving and science, before moving into information technology and becoming an advisory teacher for information technology. He regularly publishe articles and presents papers at conferences on education and information technology

Steven Russell worked as a newspaper journalist in East Anglia for more than ten year before turning towards primary school teaching as a more satisfying and rewarding career. He is now studying for a Bachelor of Education degree at Anglia Polytechnic University, at Brentwood in Essex. His media links have not been totally severed however, as he also runs a publicity, copywriting and public relations agency from his home in a village near Ipswich.

As a journalist, Steven progressed from general reporter to specialist health corres pondent, sub-editor and chief reporter, finally spending more than three years heading a forty-strong team as news editor of the East Anglian Daily Times – a regional paper selling more than 50,000 copies a day across Suffolk and north Essex.

Grace Woodford is an Advisory Teacher with the London Borough of Redbridge. She has vast experience of teaching at Key Stages 1 and 2. Grace regularly works alongside teachers in their classrooms and provides INSET courses both in and outside the Borough. Her special interests are control technology and the use of information technology in science.

Grace sits on a number of national committees and is an external examiner for the Anglia Polytechnic University and the University of Greenwich. Her publication include a chapter in *Spreading the Word* (1993) and co-authoring *Using Control IT with the Redbridge Control Box* (1988).

List of Abbreviations

APU	Assessment of Performance Unit
CATE	Council for the Accreditation of Teacher Education
CDT	Craft, design and technology
DES	Department of Education and Science
EC	European Community
ERA	Education Reform Act
ESG	Education Support Grant
GCSE	General Certificate of Secondary Education
HMI	Her Majesty's Inspectorate
INSET	Inservice Education of Teachers
IT	Information technology
LEA	Local Education Authority
LMS	Local Management of Schools
MEP	Micro Electronics Programme
NCC	National Curriculum Council
NCET	National Council for Educational Technology
NUT	National Union of Teachers
OFSTED	Office for Standards in Education
SACRE	Standing Advisory Council on Religious Education
SATS	Standard Assessment Tasks
SCAA	School Curriculum and Assessment Authority

Chapter 1

Introduction

Jon Griffin

Currently there is a sad lack of texts on information technology as applied to the primary classroom. Most of the texts that are available were written in the mid-1980s and tend to be software specific rather than addressing the educational and pedagogical issues that underpin the use of this technology in the classroom. Furthermore, preliminary research into what has been written about the effects of new technologies and delivery systems in teacher education shows that little relevant literature is available. It is not difficult to speculate why this might be the case. It might reflect the emergence of this area as a new topic for research and the lack of awareness within the teaching profession, and particularly with teacher educators, of the potential for the use of 'new technologies' within the teaching and learning situation. It might also reflect the fact that with recent innovations in information technology, powerful computers and associated software have become available to schools and universities at a relatively low cost. It also reflects the fact that teachers have not yet had opportunities either to use this technology or to appreciate its true potential.

Whatever the cause of this lack of research and literature, this book goes some way to addressing this need. It is aimed at teacher educators, teachers, and student teachers in the primary sector, attempts to be forward-looking, and addresses educational and pedagogical issues appertaining to the use of computers in the primary classroom.

As a co-editor of this book, it was my responsibility to brief the other contributors and to provide a coherence between the various chapters. All of the authors were given the same challenge, in that their chapter had to outline their vision of the computerized primary classroom in the year 2010. They were also asked to take into account their former experiences, their current involvement in information technology, the requirements of the National Curriculum, and finally they were asked to look to the future to see where all of this was leading.

The responses were interesting and varied, and in all cases provided insights into the place of information technology in the classrooms of tomorrow. Whilst most contributors kept information technology, as an issue, at the forefront of their thinking and then related the associated issues to it, Andy Lambert did the reverse. He took the issue of the 'multicultural classroom of the future' to the forefront of his thinking and kept the use of information technology to the background. However the contributors addressed their vision of the computerized classroom in the year 2010 I am sure that you will find their responses interesting, stimulating, and cogently put, and that it will give you much to think about.

As Les and I reviewed the chapters, he commented that the street that Andy Lambert described could easily be one near his home. My thoughts were turned to the town where I was born and in which there are many such streets. I then moved on to thinking about a village school near where I now live, in which at a first glance one would think that the school was free from these issues, but a second and third glance would reveal that the diversity within the school is based on religion rather than on colour or race. Thus, Andy Lambert's comments are relevant to all of us, especially if we are considering the classroom of tomorrow rather than the classroom of today.

The last ten years has been a period of constant change within our schools. We have seen a devolution of power to schools, the development of the National Curriculum, the introduction of assessment and monitoring systems, and changes at an ever faster pace. Indeed, keeping up with the changes is an almost impossible task. It is also hard to believe that it was only ten years ago that the first computers were being introduced into our primary schools.

Those early years provided some stability for teachers in the field of information technology. The number of types of computers to be found in schools was limited. BBC[1] and Research Machines[2] were the most common computers to be found in schools. And, typically, a Local Authority would decide which of these a school should purchase. The Local Authority was able to exercise control by refusing to maintain and support other systems. Now that schools have financial control over their affairs local authorities are finding it more and more difficult to insist on any one policy, and with the plethora of computer systems that are now available the decision about which one to buy gets more and more difficult. This early period was also the time during which the Micro Electronics Programme was working at its best and when the Micro Electronics Programme's National Primary Project introduced a number of resources for infant and junior schools (1985a–c).

Early computer users were brave pioneers, and they spent much of their time dealing with the intricacies of the machine – they loved meddling, and seemed more concerned about how the computer worked than with what it could do for them and how it could simplify tasks and make life easier. Today users are in the main only interested in using the computer to complete some predetermined task such as producing a document, accessing data, or using a spreadsheet to model some system in order to determine the effects as various parameters are changed. In schools we are concerned with our role as educators and learners, and with the processes that take place as our children explore and investigate their way around the computer.

There is a vast gulf between the reality of the classroom and the best use of this technology. For some teachers (and lecturers) the use of information technology is threatening and too demanding of their time and energies. This is further exacerbated by the fact that:

- they are under-trained in the use of the computer;
- the computer never seems to work when it is needed most;

- the computer needs a lot of time and effort for the user to come to grips with new software;
- computer technology is continually changing, and as a consequence staff are forced back into the situation of having to spend a lot of time and effort in understanding new computers and new software;
- there is just not enough time in the day to do all that a busy teacher needs to do or would like to do.

Hales and Russell (ch. 8) confirm this view when they quote a friend who says:

> . . . [the computer] spent a month sitting on a trolley. *No one has yet had the time* to work out what it can do, review the software and tell the staff how good it is, or otherwise. Generally, I would say that a third of our teachers . . . are very intimidated and a bit frightened by computers, and really need some help in overcoming that fear before they can turn to teaching anything substantial. Others who are more broad-minded are not scared by computers, but *just can't find the time* to spend a day sitting in front of a screen to find out what they could use for a class. [my emphasis]

I regularly hear these comments, in one form or another, as I visit schools. While supervising a student on her second teaching practice recently, I commented that a particular year one boy might benefit by using the computer to word process some of his work. The response was that the school's word-processing package had not been working for some time (the first two weeks of the teaching practice and the preceding period of observation) and another was on order. By the end of the practice the school had still not received the word-processing package, thus to my knowledge no word processing had been done in the school for nine weeks – how were the requirements of the National Curriculum for information technology (DES, 1989c) being delivered?[3]

Another student, in line with school practice, locked the computer away on a Friday evening and did not get it out until the Wednesday or Thursday of the following week, thus the children were only able to gain access to the computer for less than half of the week – I was able to do something about this, but only for the duration of the teaching practice.

I was concerned by a recent conversation with my children. They are clearly not quite so lucky as Stephen Heppell's (ch. 10). When asked:

Question: What did you do at school today?

After the 'grunt', the response was:

Answer: I was told that I couldn't hand in my Religious Education project in its word-processed form. I've got to hand it in, in my best handwriting – all 10,000 words!

Question: Why is that?

Answer: Because they won't believe I wrote it if it is word processed . . .

Who is to say that the pupil who hand-writes an essay did not copy it? More importantly, our children are being prevented from writing in an environment that enables them to develop their work in a non-linear way, that enables their work to evolve, be reviewed and edited without the pain of rewriting it after each draft. Of course handwriting is important and has its place near the centre of the curriculum, but the 'extended' essay is the wrong time and the wrong place to work at this skill.

Answer: . . . and when we are allowed to use the computer (I am still waiting for
the 'when' to happen), we mustn't use the dictionary, thesaurus, grammar checker . . .

Why? I ask myself.

We have similar problems at the University. One lecturer told students not to word
process an essay (when it was a requirement) because she did not 'believe' in
computers; another would not mark some assignments which related to the use of
information technology in her subject area because she felt ill-equipped to do this;
others have just quietly retired. Universities and colleges involved in teacher training
need to ensure that *all* their staff are familiar with new technologies and are capable of
using computers in the classroom. They need to appreciate how the use of computers
affects teaching and learning, particularly in their own subject.

I have long believed that a subject specialist *does more good and is more effective* if
they state at the beginning of a lesson that they are not very good with computers, and
then use them in their teaching, than they do by getting a computer expert to show
students how a computer is used in, say, English or mathematics or science or
whatever. This latter strategy sends all the wrong signals to our students, not least of
which is that 'Computers have no real role to play in the teaching of x.' How much more
'good' is done when the subject specialist is also an expert in the use of computers
within their subject area?

In citing a small but significant minority of teachers and lecturers, I would not like the
reader to think that all teachers and lecturers are like this. The vast majority of teachers
are trying hard to cope with ever-changing computer technology, the information
explosion, and with the consequential effect that these have on teaching and learning.

> With the eyes of a child
> You must come out and see
> That your world's spinning round
> And through life you will be
> A small part of a hope of a love that exists
> In the eyes of a child you will see.
> (Lodge, 1969)

This chorus is a reminder that through 'the eyes of a child' computers and the
associated technologies are simple and a part of their everyday life, and for the rest of
us it seems that 'our world is spinning round' with the rate of change and growth in this
area. We as teachers often get 'bogged down' with the technology and sometimes
forget that while our pupils may be more familiar with computers, we as educators are
competent and have a lot to offer when it comes to teaching and learning. In unfamiliar
but non-computer environments we would have no problems in appraising the situation and 'stretching' our pupils – so it is with computers, with a little confidence we can
leave the technology to the children and get on with the teaching and learning.

As we look around, we see that

> . . . the development of information technology is changing the home and the workplace.
> Its impact on the lives of individuals and on the economy continues to grow, and it is
> essential that pupils can take advantage of its opportunities and understand its effects.
> Adults are still coming to terms with information technology; children take it for granted
> and are excited by its possibilities.[4] Information technology in the National Curriculum

will harness that excitement and will enable young people to use its power to meet the needs of the future.
(Department of Education and Science, 1990)

In essence the National Curriculum for information technology means that our pupils will be able to use computers to handle and manipulate text, images and sound.[5] Furthermore, our pupils are also required to use information technology to invest-igate.[6] In the context of information technology the activities relating to the phrase 'to investigate' are:

- measurement and control;
- modelling.

Many of these issues are taken up later in the book (text, images and sound in chs 7–10; measurement and control in chs 5–6). Other issues, including children (ch. 2), teaching and learning (ch. 9), the classroom (chs 5–6), cultural diversity (ch. 4), observing the common themes around the world in information technology (the manipulation of text, sound and images, the use of word processors, databases and spreadsheets, and the impact on teaching styles) by comparing the United Kingdom with the United States of America and the Hashemite Kingdom of Jordan (ch. 3), and the future of learning (ch. 10), are also addressed – these both weave their way through the book and are addressed separately within it.

Although discussed more fully later in the book, it would seem appropriate briefly to discuss the issues relating to 'handling and manipulating text, images and sound' as well as those of 'using information technology to investigate'.

Teachers often comment that they have a limited supply of software and use that as an excuse for not doing very much work on the computer with their children. The reality, of course, is that teachers need only a 'handful' of software. In essence they need a word processor, database, spreadsheet, Logo, and control technology pack-ages. At this point I intend to focus on the use of word processors, databases and spreadsheets.

If we look at the National Curriculum, we see that all children should be taught that 'information technology can be used to help plan and organize ideas in written and graphical form' (DES, 1990). This statement underpins the word-processing activities that our pupils must undertake. In the past ten to twenty years, word processors have progressed from text editors, through word processors to sophisticated desk-top publishing systems that can handle both text and images, and allow the writer to consider page design and layout as part of the writing process. Facilities such as spell checkers, grammar checkers, a thesaurus and word count are now included as standard features in modern word processors. How are we going to use these to free our pupils as they embark on the writing process? I have already mentioned schools who have banned these features from being used. From visits to California and Illinois in the United States of America I have observed that it is a requirement that these features are used. Indeed, dominant computer-based activity carried out in American schools is word processing. In this country our pupils use word processors for 50 per cent (HMI, 1991) of the time spent on computers – this is a lot of time! It is sad that 75 per cent (HMI, 1991) of those pupils word processing in this country are only doing a 'best copy' of their work. Indeed, many packages now have text (word-processing) facilities with them, for example: paint and draw programs.

If some of the obstacles to pupils becoming writers include spelling, presentation, grammar and content, then the modern word processor has a place in overcoming these. In the first instance the writer is 'freed' from the constraints of 'poor' spelling and grammar and can concentrate on writing. The word processor frees the pupil from having to write in a linear fashion – it allows the writer to put down his or her thoughts as they come, and to reorganize them later. The ability to reorganize, insert, edit and correct text with ease enables pupils to concentrate on the content and improves the quality of their work. It is this improvement that leads some teachers to believe that the work has not been done by the pupil, and to these teachers banning the use of word processors and the features within them. A real bonus with word-processed work is that, as a consequence of the high quality of work and presentation, 'self-esteem' rises, particularly of those pupils whose presentation skills are lacking for one reason or another. In preparing for lectures with our first-year BEd students, Heppell and Millwood highlighted some emerging issues for the use of word processors, these include:

- classroom organization and management;
- appropriate strategies for developing writing skills;
- different hardware and software systems – how do teachers and pupils move easily from one to another?
- what do we mean by finished?
- what is the impact of spelling and grammar checkers?
- text as a part of the learning environment – what is its role now?

(UltraLab, 1994)

It is not my intention to answer these questions. I leave them with you for you to discuss and share with your colleagues.

Information-handling is another important area of the curriculum, and currently there are a number of good database programs around. Some key questions are:

- what is a database?
- what is their use in schools?
- how does the computer add to the quality of teaching and learning?

Simply, a database is an organized file of information which can be about people, plants, animals, objects, etc. We are all familiar with the 'filing cabinet' and understand its concepts. We equally understand that if information is filed in the cabinet in an orderly fashion, then its retrieval is straightforward. So it is with databases. The significant differences being, (a) one is a paper system (filing cabinet) and the other is an electronic system; and (b) the speed at which information can be retrieved from the system.

For pupils gathering data, organizing it into information and asking questions about it is an important part of their learning. Where the data is limited, probably the best way to handle it is manually. However, as the amounts of data collected grow, the need for a computer system increases in order for the children to be able to handle the information. The use of the data requires the children to be able to look for patterns guess relationships, and to form hypotheses. In solving a hypothesis, a computer database can be used to sort the data by any criteria, to ask 'What if . . . ' questions, and to draw graphs, and where appropriate the hypothesis can be modified.

I have an interest in genealogy, and keep my family file on a database. For a family activity I printed the data in a number of ways. Figure 1.1 shows a subset of my file sorted by date of birth. The subset of my family file contains five fields, namely: Surname; Given Names; Date of Birth; County (of Birth); and Gender.

Surname	Given Names	Date of Birth	County	Gender
GRIFFIN	William	1781	Kent	Male
PENGELLY	Roger	1803	Devon	Male
PENGELLY	Elizabeth	1807	Devon	Female
GRIFFIN	Emanuel	1811	Kent	Male
GRIFFIN	Jane Susanna	1811	Kent	Female
TALBOT	Joseph	1812	Somerset	Male
TALBOT	Esther	1816	Somerset	Female
PENGELLY	Grace	1829	Devon	Female
TALBOT	Walter	1838	Somerset	Male
BENTLEY	Ellen	1839	Sussex	Female
FRANCIS	Thomas	1844	Somerset	Male
TALBOT	Eliza	1844	Somerset	Female
EDGECOMBE	Elizabeth	1848	Somerset	Female
PENGELLY	Elizabeth A	1849	Devon	Female
COOPER	Mary Elizabeth	1854	Lincolnshire	Female
THEAKER	Alfred	1856	Lincolnshire	Male
TALBOT	Charlotte	1865	Somerset	Female
TALBOT	Arthur Hugh	1866	Somerset	Male
FRANCIS	Charlotte Ann	1870	Somerset	Female
GRIFFIN	William	1873	Kent	Male

Figure 1.1 *A printout of a subset of my family file: sorted by date of birth.*

I also printed the file by Surname, County (of Birth) and Gender. These outputs, along with the other outputs that were generated, including a family tree, enabled my family to review our ancestors and learn much about our family history.

Another powerful, content-free tool is the spreadsheet.[7] In the world of commerce and industry the spreadsheet is a tool used by decision-makers. Its power lies in the ability of the computer to do rapid calculations in conjunction with a formal statement relating one variable or cell to another. It is probably the least understood of the generic tools (word processor, database and spreadsheet) used in the primary classroom, and as such probably needs a simple example to illustrate its function and potential. The following example (figures 1.2, 1.3 and 1.4) illustrates the use of a spreadsheet for calculating the costs relating to two shopping trips on 2 and 8 August 1994.

Figure 1.2 illustrates the layout of a simple spreadsheet and shows the use of a range of data types (date, text, number and currency). The essential processes of computer modelling are to:

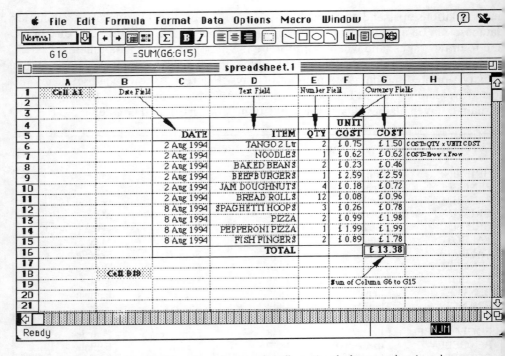

Figure 1.2   *Example of a spreadsheet for a shopping list: illustrating the layout and various data types.*

- *identify the variables:* In this case, the quantity (QTY) and unit cost (UNIT COST) There are of course other variables, which, although they do not affect the result of the calculations, are important for the added information and meaning that they give to the spreadsheet. In this case, the date of purchase (DATE) and the description of the item (ITEM) purchased are two examples.
- *find the relationship[s]:* In this case there are two. The first is the relationship between the quantity bought and the unit cost, which gives the actual cost (COST and can be found by the multiplying QTY by UNIT COST. The second is the tota cost of the shopping, and can be found by calculating the sum of the individua COSTs (SUM(G6:G15)).
- *evaluate the results:* Looking at the results enables us to use them to make decisions In this case I only have £13.00, so I will have to rethink the items that I buy. Thi process will also include asking 'What if . . .' questions, such as, 'What if I only buy one bottle of Tango?' Figure 1.3 shows the results of this change on the corresponding COST and on the total cost – by changing the data in one cell, corresponding calculations are carried out instantly.[8]

Figure 1.4 shows the hidden formulae (relationships) contained within the spreadshee that enable these 'What if . . .' questions to be answered.

The use of the spreadsheet is not just limited to shopping lists. Other examples of it use might include the analysis of weather data and looking for relationships, such as, 'I the speed we run related to the length of our legs?'

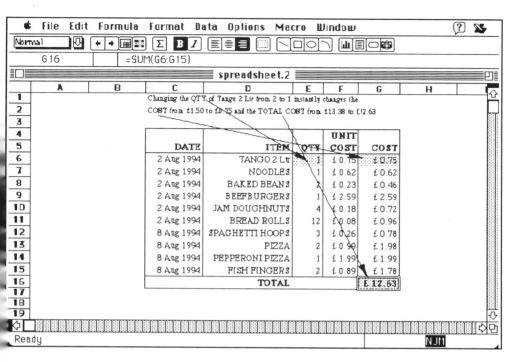

'igure 1.3 *The effect of changing the quantity [QTY] of Tango from 2 to 1 on the spreadsheet.*

The power of the spreadsheet as a learning tool lies in the rapid calculation offered in :onjunction with a clear, formal representation of the relationship between variables. This ' . . . match[es] both the desire for an increasingly child-centred learning environ-ment and the perceived need for guided discovery learning to play a greater part in the :ducation process' (UltraLab, 1994).

In addition, the ease with which relationships between variables can be established :nables pupils to observe changes as they enter data. In the above example, the cost of)ne bottle of Tango was seen instantaneously, as was the change to the total cost of the hopping. In another example, during the analysis of weather data, the average :emperature would be updated as each entry was made.

The use of spreadsheets for modelling enables our pupils, at an early age, to work vith and handle numerical relationships. They also enable our pupils to achieve hought processes that will be useful to them in problem-solving activities.

In looking at word processors, databases and spreadsheets, I have briefly covered hree of the most significant applications for use in primary schools. In doing so I have :mphasized the teaching and learning. The use of information technology could and hould make a difference to the way that we learn, but all too often we focus on the echnology – this is not surprising when we find all our time taken up with the intricacies)f loading, running, copying, fixing and setting up the computer. Finally, there is one nore change that we are likely to miss – that is the change in ourselves:

> However, to focus only on the technology is to miss another key change that schools . . .
> miss at their peril: change in people. As we move further into the 'Information Age' we are

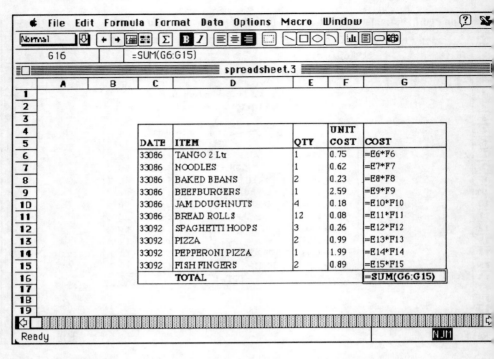

Figure 1.4 *The hidden formulae (relationships) contained within the spreadsheet.*

changing our habits, our capabilities and most important of all, we are changing our expectations. Whilst we have watched computers in home, school and business develop over the last two decades, the computers have 'watched' us develop even faster; typically, the younger we are, the more rapidly we have changed. This is fundamentally important and poorly understood.
(Heppell, 1993)

The use of information technology should make a difference to teaching and learning. One problem for us is how to take advantage of this high level of skill that our pupils have, as Heppell once said: 'What we seem to be observing is the Andy Pandy generation leading the Sonic generation into the information age, and the Andy Pandy generation have some homework to do . . . ' (Heppell, 1993). Thus this book attempts to raise our awareness of the use of information technology in the learning environment and to discuss some of the key issues.

NOTES

1. The BBC model B and BBC Master computers.
2. The 380Z, 480Z and Nimbus range of computers.
3. See also SCAA, 1994, esp. p. 3 ('in a variety of forms, including combining *text*, graphics [images] and sound').
4. E.g., the sentiment given in Lodge, 1969.

5. See ch. 8 for a forward-looking and innovative way of handling text, images and sound. See also SCAA, 1994, esp. p. 3 ('in a variety of forms, including combining *text*, graphics [images] and sound').
6. See SCAA, 1994, esp. p. 3 ('using IT to investigate').
7. A content-free tool is a computer program that allows the user to have control over its content. These programs include word processors, databases and spreadsheets.
8. See UltraLab (1994b), course notes.

Chapter 2

Children, Computers and Contradictions

Leslie Bash

As co-editor of this volume, this writer may be reasonably expected to display h
credentials in the field of information technology and primary education, but he has t
admit that they are virtually non-existent. As an education 'theorist' working in
university, his credentials as a classroom practitioner are probably not much bette
except that he has recently had the privilege of working on full-time secondment in
north London junior school for a term. Although having young children of his ow
and having been a visitor to primary schools for many years on teaching practic
supervision, the experience of being in regular, close contact with a large number of
to 11-year-olds over a period of some months was a rather different propositio
Importantly, it resulted in a challenge to some taken-for-granted ideas and ha
prompted a degree of questioning. Also, given involvement in a good deal of staffroo
banter as well as more focused discussion with individual classroom teachers, there wa
the opportunity to reflect upon various dimensions of the context of learning an
intellectual progress.

After a good deal of consideration, a conviction remained that there was a prevailin
commonsense view of primary school age children which is locked into a crud
unreconstructed developmental psychology. No amount of evidence from the clas
room or elsewhere appears to challenge the assumption that young children are at
particular stage in their intellectual development, with only a limited capacity to gras
what are seen as complex abstract ideas. Accordingly, the smooth, upward progressio
from infancy is seen to be checked only by lack of external stimulation or by congenit
disabilities. It is still commonplace to find parents using 'baby' talk with their ver
young offspring on the unspoken assumption that such verbal intercourse is ag
appropriate and that 'adult' talk should be postponed until a later stage. Th
assumption is also to be seen in the objects given to children as playthings and a
explicit tools for learning. Preferences for graded reading schemes and strictly sequer
tial maths programmes predate the counter-progressive era in education policy of th
last decades of the twentieth century.

However, those who have spent any significant period of time interacting with youn
children will have noticed that such assumptions are frequently misplaced. Unremark

ably, early experiences are characterized by all kinds of complexities and contradictions, such that it is not always possible to plan and predict the intellectual progress of children, a fact not unfamiliar to the primary classroom teacher! On the other hand, teachers have managed to retain a degree of control over the pedagogy of the primary classroom and to convince themselves that they have complete knowledge of their children's intellectual development. To a large extent, this may be seen to be linked to a knowledge and control of conventional educational technology. Chalk, paper, pencils, books – and even electronic media such as the video – are in the final analysis within the framework of existing practice of the vast majority of educational professionals.

The computer has, seemingly, challenged much of this. The structure of pedagogic discourse, as Bernstein (1990) has put it, is now viewed as highly problematic, since we may need to think afresh about the manner in which the business of education is enacted in the classroom. It can be argued fairly convincingly that, for example, a piece of chalk carries with it no particular form of discourse until the teacher begins to write with it on the blackboard. Only then does the process of pedagogy take place, with its attendant assumptions of a conventional classroom structure (teacher holding sway over a group of children); and, likewise, when children put pen to paper. But the meanings generated in the course of conventional educational practice cannot be assumed in the context of the computer.

Why is this? Possibly it has something to do with the lack of knowledge regarding the computer and its operations on the part of the teacher, and thus an alteration in the dynamics of the classroom. To put it another way, '. . . control over the production and transmission of "new knowledge" about computing is likely to be the site of struggle' (Singh, 1993, p. 43). Yet, such a struggle might well be resolved in terms of conventional gender differences as the discourse centres upon 'technocratic masculinity' and the consequential legitimation of computing skills (Bernstein, 1990, p. 43). If this is true, it suggests that the acceptance of the computer in the primary classroom may be dependent upon assumed cultural norms of behaviour, both of teachers and of children.

Above all, computer discourse is 'future' orientated: the past is stretched so that last year is seen as part of a completely different era in the history of information technology; the twenty-first century is upon the horizon – and the year 2010 beckons. In terms of world history, the next two decades are a brief moment, but in the context of technological change and, even more pertinently, in the era of the personal computer, twenty years represents the possibility of profound transformations in human potential. As ever, a significant contradiction stands out: older members of society, having lived through much change, are more likely to resist further change than younger people whose life experience is somewhat shorter. Children, it would seem, have taken the information technology revolution in their stride. Added to that, the computer is as much a part of the internal architecture of the primary school classroom as the blackboard and the reading corner.

The speed with which young children are apparently able to accommodate – even embrace – technological change raises an interesting issue regarding the nature of the relationship between the teacher and the taught. After all, children are supposed to be subordinates in the process of education, and even if they are not treated entirely as a *tabulae rasae* they still ought not to be more knowledgeable than their teachers! As a consequence, the issue of computers in the primary classroom extends beyond the technical competence of the teacher to the very basis of the teacher's profession: identity.

It should be clear by now that the approach taken in this chapter to the theme of computing in the English primary school is somewhat contentious, viewing it essentially as a cultural phenomenon rather than in terms of technical accretion. Indeed, it the perspective of the technical which needs to be subjected to some scrutiny, since suggests a secret garden to which entry is only gained as a result of possession of ke instructional knowledge. Accordingly, the author makes no apologies for suggestin the adoption of a critical position on culture, education and technology in general – an information technology in particular. As we have already seen, there are som fundamental contradictions in the discourse regarding the interaction between childre and computer technology, and it is unlikely that there is yet to be anything like consistent approach to this area of children's experience. These contradictions ar manifested in numerous ways: the insistence on the centrality of information techno logy to the core curriculum while many teachers remain, at best, indifferent t computers in the classroom, and, at worst, completely computer-phobic; the emphas on the creative use of computers as against the 'non-creative' aspect of game machines; and so on.

We are, arguably, at a transitional stage in Western technological culture. We ma have travelled beyond the early phases of industrialization, and yet not reached an er when the culture of 'scientific technology' has entered the very core of our fundament; thinking and assumptions. By adding 'scientific' to 'technology' there is the evocatio of a broader context of intellectual endeavour, of being guided by principles and c reflection upon rational considerations. On the other hand, there is a sense in whic 'technicism' has penetrated much of social life, suggesting that human problems hav obvious, rational solutions and therefore do not merit any kind of debate in terms c values or ideologies. Notions of efficiency replace awkward questions such as whethe from an ethical or political standpoint, a particular course of action ought or ought nc to be taken. In many computer programs – and, of course, in many computer games any ethical/political parameters have already been drawn and the operator/gamester obliged to follow the rules. We are indebted to a number of contemporary thinker; notably Jürgen Habermas (1971), for drawing our attention to the ideologies built int the very structure of technology. That is to say, it is not that the manner of soci; interaction is driven by the nature of the technology, but rather that the technolog itself is shaped by social considerations.

The relationship between education and technology is complex, but none the less c some antiquity. Moreover, the specific connection with information technology ha been of continual importance, ever since children were required to reproduce the thoughts, ideas and knowledge in some kind of permanent or semi-permanent form The path from chalk and slate, through exercise book and pencil, to word processor : not a particularly long one, although it seems obvious that what was asked of th elementary schoolchild of Victorian times appears far removed from that asked of th primary pupil of today. The point is, however, that some use of technology wa invariably required in the execution of learning tasks, while the question remains as t the very manner in which the technology of any one era shapes or constrair educational endeavour.

This leads inevitably to the core issue: the domination of human action by a disembodied technology, the onward march of the 'technological imperative'. Even those who would dispute such a notion, having sufficient faith in the ability of human beings to control their lives, tremble before the power of the computer games machine's apparent ability to take over the minds and souls of their offspring like some alien presence. The discourse in relation to artificial intelligence suggests a future in which humanity, in its quest to facilitate greater control over life, submits, as the ultimate irony, to rule by computer. On the other hand, a fine rhetoric is frequently heard regarding the computer as a tool – a sophisticated one, it is admitted – but nevertheless a device to enhance human capability and to release latent aptitudes. However, this is predicated upon an assumption that technology can always be subordinated, in a rational manner, to articulated individual demands and social processes. The digitized character of the computer in particular has challenged the assumption that technological change can be gradually and smoothly integrated into existing cultural practices. The 'friendliness' of technology depends upon the presence of 'analogue' devices which enable human beings to make appropriate connections with their taken-for-granted world.

In the eyes of a considerable number of teachers, of many parents, and of adults in general, information technology appears to impose an order demanding a kind of obedience in the acceptance of a functional *status quo*. There is an awareness of the danger of the means coming to define the ends, where human goals are adjusted to the available technological media and where technological norms appear as central human values. Thus, the goal of communication might be translated as a demand for telephones, or facsimile machines; or music appreciation is seen as the ownership of a compact disc player. In the case of the computer, the kind of end results desired may have to be defined in terms of the available software – and, as programs develop, so goals are altered. The upshot is that the structure of technical achievements largely determines what may be viewed as core educational aims.

Yet part of the very attraction of computer technology is in its mystery, its magical properties, its status as a totem. There is more than a hint of conspicuous consumption here: the desktop computer having pride of place in the office, the classroom, or the home. However, there is the question of the extent to which the potential user of the computer was able to do anything other than switch the machine on and off. Yet, it was clear that the forward march of progress was not to be halted and the issue of information technology in schools was to have national significance as seen in the stated official policy by the UK government on computing and education. Since the early 1980s, the aim has been to ensure access of all children to computer technology; and its incorporation into the core of the National Curriculum has secured its place as the symbol of progress of an advanced industrial nation. Among educationists, a highly charged vocabulary has evolved, so that, 'whenever computers are discussed, words such as "revolution", "powerful ideas", "microworlds", and "student empowerment" occur frequently' (Miller and Olson, 1994, p. 122).

One of the major difficulties in this area surrounds the contradictory approach to technology manifested in the national culture. Whereas at one time a new technology might be universally hailed either as a solution to longstanding problems or else as opening up futures as yet hardly conceived, continuing and sometimes growing alienation within a context of what some might label as 'postmodernism' presents a rather more confused picture. The building of the Channel Tunnel, linking Britain t mainland Europe, unleashed a host of nostalgic sentiments, if not outright xenophob and Anglocentrism. The prospect of a high-speed rail connection between Paris ar London stands in contrast to the more leisurely 'outmoded' means of travel via cros channel ferry. Thus, with the computer, there are suspicions that human life increasingly directed by a technology which has taken on a momentum of its own.

On the other hand, despite its popular appeal, the above perspective suggests a lac of sophistication in current thinking. Not least, the generation gap is showin, Notwithstanding the well-documented, narrowly nationalistic behaviour of mar young Britons when on holiday in mainland Europe, there would appear to be a greate propensity among children, certainly when compared with their parents, to perceiv themselves as Europeans. A parallel might be suggested with technology, especial computers, where similar attitudes prevail. For all the lure of the games machine, the is still excitement at being able to use the computer to give expression to artistic idea at being able to experiment with text and design – in short, it has the potential t expand learning opportunities beyond current expectations.

The year 2010 holds a promise. The fulfilment of that promise depends largely c fundamental cultural change which, at one and the same time, leads to the destructic of the barrier between the 'humanities' and 'science/technology' and to the empowe ment of the young. An important dimension of such cultural change lies in th preparation of the next generation of primary school teachers. This may have rathe less to do with the practical application of information technology in the classroon crucial though that is, than with the raising of cultural awareness. For too lon; scientific and technological activities have been seen as not merely beyond th capabilities of many primary school teachers, but also beyond the remit of primar education. The National Curriculum, if it has done little else, has raised the profiles c these areas and has required teachers to demonstrate appropriate competence in th classroom. On the other hand, teachers are not empty vessels waiting to be filled wit new and exotic pedagogical cargo: it is somewhat unrealistic, and perhaps a litt. dangerous, to expect them to be ready to take on board innovation simply because particular lobby has been persuasive in its mission, albeit with rational argument.

If teachers are professionals, it means that they already possess a body of theory an practice, and it is this latter which is significant for the future of computers in th primary classroom, since 'it is important to understand teachers' practice in deta because it is that practice and its history that allows us to understand how teachers us technology – how they incorporate new tools and new symbols into their teachir culture' (Miller and Olson, 1994, p. 123).

We may be in some danger of attributing Luddite characteristics to teachers wh have failed to take on board information technology in the classroom, whereas a mor accurate view might be that there is a failure to bridge the cultural divide. Moreove this cultural divide has been exacerbated by many of the recent changes wrought upc the profession which have served to de-skill teachers. There may be little point i exhorting teachers to become more computer-minded in an era of bureaucratize curriculum 'delivery' and testing. The more likely outcome is that information techno logy is subject to the process of commodification whereby teachers see it as somethir which has to be given space in the primary curriculum as a consequence of centr. government policy, but, if possible, loaded on to somebody else's shoulders – th information technology 'specialist'. In this case, information technology retains its mystique, and other teachers feel justified in not having their lack of expertise challenged.

After well over a decade of the presence of the BBC microcomputer in English primary classrooms, its acceptance as an item of furniture is taken for granted. Unlike the video machine, which itself has posed the occasional technical difficulty for the user, it cannot be used to entertain a passive audience; the computer demands active engagement if it is not to become a redundant electronic gadget. The sometimes separate worlds of the teacher and the child must converge in a manner which is conducive to learning, in order to overcome the cultural barriers to educational advance.

Chapter 3

It's the Same the World Over

Jon Griffin

Like many technological devices, such as the video, the computer always seems to go wrong when one most needs it to work. It would seem that the computer has a mind of its own! It knows how we feel, and plays on us. It would seem that the computer always fails to operate when we need it to work, but that it always works for other people. This is not the case! For most of us the computer is reliable. Of course there are times for all of us when it will not work. There are times it lets us down, and dealing with the computer under pressure is sometimes difficult. Many teachers in primary classrooms lack expertise and experience, and thus the computer is a real threat. It doesn't help us to realize that we are without the expertise that we require – we, in our teaching, are used to being in control and being ahead of our pupils in their learning, and not, as is often the case with computers, being behind them. For in many classrooms it is the children who are the real experts.

Thus, when we think about these pressures and problems we consider that we are alone. The realities are that many other teachers within our own school, in schools across the country, and in schools around the world, are feeling the same pressures and have the same problems.

The truth of the matter is that we have made tremendous progress since the early 1980s, when computers were first introduced into primary classrooms.[1] In those days we had the Micro Electronics Programme to support us, and in particular we had the Micro Electronics Programme Primary Project.[2] This project provided teachers with a great deal of material (1984, 1985 a–d) for use in the classroom and was a catalyst for many of the innovations that took place in the middle and late 1980s, and provided a 'kick start' to the use of computers in the primary sector. Since those days computers have increased in power and capacity and the software has improved beyond all recognition. We have moved from using subject-specific software to content-free packages that enable the needs of individual pupils to be more directly addressed. Software is becoming more 'user-friendly' and powerful. We are moving from using word processors such as Folio (which, although dated, were extremely good in their day) to fully-fledged word processors such as Word,[3] databases, and spreadsheets. The power that is now at our fingertips is quite fantastic – the problems are, 'How do we harness it?' and 'How do we use it' to the benefit of our children?

In those days we also had advisory teachers and advisory teams dedicated to supporting our teachers in schools across a whole range of subjects, including information technology. Now, with the changes in education and the lack of money available for this work, more and more teachers are finding themselves on their own. In areas like information technology this poses serious problems for our schools. Despite all these problems, computers offer us tremendous benefits in the learning environment, and it is the use of the computer to promote learning that interests me most.

Over the last decade we have gained a great deal of expertise in using computers in the learning environment. This expertise has been recognized by others around the world and has been used by governments as they have introduced computers into their schools.

The Jordan Experience

One example of this recognition was the Computers in Education in Jordan project.[4] This project was important in two ways. The first being that it was one of the largest computer projects in the developing world and that it provided a model for other projects to follow. The second, and probably the most important reason, was that it led and informed the educational reforms that were taking place in the Hashemite Kingdom of Jordan.

'The roots of the rationale which now underpins the Computers in Education [in Jordan] Project can be seen in the problems and issues recognised to be facing the Jordanian education system in 1987' (McMahon, 1990). The project was based on the Micro Electronics Programme and incorporated the support systems similar to those previously offered by advisory teams in the United Kingdom. A Computer Education Directorate was set up. This body reported directly to the Ministry of Education and contained three divisions; namely: software development, technical support, and curriculum development. A steering group known as the National Team[5] was also established to advise both the Ministry of Education and the Computer Education Directorate. Thus this initiative had support at the highest levels.

There were those who wanted a technically based curriculum, while others of us wanted, and obtained, a curriculum based on educational principles which considered the cross-curricular issues relating to computing.

As within the National Curriculum, the key activities involved word processors, databases, spreadsheets, and Logo. The need for culturally based software was recognized and addressed, with the software being 'Arabized' to run in Arabic on the computers. In addition, activities were also culturally based.[6]

Like young people around the world, the Jordanian pupils have little or no fear of the technology and enjoy the lessons immensely, particularly the more practical aspects of the work. They demonstrate their enthusiasm by

> attending computer clubs in their own time and by using a variety of computer packages for enjoyment and to support the work that they are doing in other areas of the curriculum.

> The effects of this enthusiasm on the pupils' general educational development is not yet known. Despite the fact that many parents have little knowledge of computers they are supportive of the innovation.[7]

As a result of this project some 2,000 computers were obtained, software provided, and teachers trained. As in the United Kingdom, the teachers were fearful and the children fearless!

The benefits of this project to introduce computers into Jordanian classrooms have not just been about learning to use computers and their role in teaching and learning; they have gone beyond this into the wider curriculum and are impacting on the teaching methods employed in other subjects. The hold that didactic teaching methods once had has gone, there is now a (slow) move to the use of problem-solving activities and other strategies for teaching – thanks to the introduction of the computer.

A Glimpse at Computing in the USA

'One, two, three, . . . twenty-nine, thirty, thirty-one . . .'
    'Dr Griffin, how does this compare to . . .?'

My mind had been wandering as, for the third time, I tried to count how many computers there were in this resource room. I had already been shown an interactive video system which linked the whole school and beyond. I never did find out how many computers were in that room; I did, however, discover that every classroom in the school had at least two computers, and that for once the teachers were not afraid of the technology and readily accepted it in their classrooms. This had not always been the case, but adequate resourcing, training and support had done the trick. The computers were used for a range of activities, including word processing, information handling (databases), modelling (spreadsheets), and the manipulation of text, images and sound using HyperCard.

My visit to this neighbourhood elementary school in South Central Los Angeles was during the week after the riots in 1992. Many of the schools were closed, and it was difficult to appreciate fully how widespread the use of computers is in Californian schools. California has put millions of dollars into equipping schools (both elementary and high schools) with computers. In order to receive these large sums, which can be as much as $500,000, the schools have to add funds of their own and spend significant amounts of it on staff development and support. Not all schools in California or the United States are resourced to this level, although there is a tendency to create a computer laboratory (even in elementary schools) rather than to disperse the computers around the school in classrooms. Indeed, the vast majority of schools are like those in the United Kingdom, with teachers trying to do their best with limited resources and little real support. There is a more typical elementary school in Southern Illinois which I visit frequently. In this school there is one computer in each classroom and a resource room containing six computers. A visit to this school usually finds a child or small group of children seated at the computer doing some word processing.

Electronic Mail and the Global Village

The global village has arrived. It now takes a few hours to travel from one country to another, and with the use of computers and telecommunication systems it is possible to have instant communication between any two points on the earth. With television and radio we can see and hear events as they take place on the other side of the world. With the telephone, facsimile machines (fax) and computers we can communicate with loved ones and carry out our business wherever we or they might live.

By connecting a modem[8] to a computer we can communicate with other colleagues and institutions around the world. This opens up tremendous possibilities for the work that we do in the classroom. We can link with a school on the other side of the country (or the world) and get involved in joint projects. At a simple level this might involve getting to know each other, or at a more advanced level it might involve sharing data from very different areas. I use such a system for keeping in touch with colleagues around the world, and from time to time my students communicate electronically, using email, with California State University at San Marcos.[9] From these communications my students have:

- discovered that

    'the weather is hot today, about 85° Fahrenheit...'[10]

- had a request for information on teaching:

    'I am in an elementary school tomorrow, and will be teaching math[ematics] to a second grade class – Any ideas???'

- been provided with information:

    'I am fine thanks, so is everyone at San Marcos. The house shook a bit and it was worrying for a while . . . the most reliable means of communication was internet [an email system] . . . thanks for your concern [the day after the February 1994 earthquake in Los Angeles] . . .'

The use of electronic mail enables us to focus our writing with an audience in mind and for us to get a tangible response which we can act upon.

The use of email along with the more traditional use of information technology is within the framework of manipulating text, images and sounds, and among other things requires the use of word processors, databases and spreadsheets, and enables activities to be based within the wider curriculum.[11]

We worry about equipment, software, teaching strategies, whether the computer will work, budgets, staffing, curriculum developments – and the list goes on and on and on. You know, IT'S THE SAME THE WORLD OVER . . . We can only do our best.

NOTES

1. The Government's scheme to introduce microcomputers into every primary school in the country, November 1982.
2. The Micro Electronics Programme Primary Project was led by Anita Straker.
3. Microsoft Word runs on IBM compatible machines (Word for Windows) and on the Apple range of computers.

4. The Computers in Education Project in Jordan was managed by Robin Bartlett
    Lorraine Stone (Changing Perspectives Limited).
5. The National Team consisted of very senior academics and administrators.
6. For example, Logo activities were derived from mosaics found in the mosques.
7. From a conversation with Okla Khleifat, Director of the Computer Education Directora
    in 1990.
8. A modem is a device which enables a computer to be linked to the telephone system
    communications purposes.
9. Professor Peggy Kelly is my contact at California State University at San Marcos.
10. This email was received in mid-February 1993.
11. For example, English and the rest of the National Curriculum subjects.

Chapter 4

Classroom of Tomorrow

Andy Lambert

There is a road I often travel along that comprises a Chinese herbalist, Greek shipper, Saree shop, Turkish café, Punjabi suit shop, Chinese, Malay and Indian restaurants, Cypriot fish and chip shop, Italian furniture retailer, Halal butcher and an Indian grocer. This road runs between the areas of Tottenham and Muswell Hill in the compact north London borough of Haringey, where, according to the 1991 census, 29 per cent of the population were from ethnic minorities.

Haringey's population is ethnically, culturally, linguistically and religiously diverse, and the Authority welcomes this diversity. In our commitment to multicultural education, Haringey is not atypical if we consider the expectations and requirements to be found in official documents such as the Education Reform Act (DES, 1988a) and the ensuing clarification documents. For example, the Department of Education and Science circular 5/89 states: 'It is intended that the curriculum should reflect the culturally diverse society to which pupils belong . . . ' and that the foundation subjects need to include . . . coverage across the curriculum of gender and multicultural issues' (DES, 1989a). Later in the same year Department of Education and Science circular 16/89 explained that 'A school is better equipped to offer each child suitable education if the basic facts about his or her cultural identity – including ethnic origin, linguistic background, and religion – are known' (DES, 1989b). The National Curriculum Council (NCC) in its 1990 guidance document on the whole curriculum specifies that

> introducing multicultural perspectives gives pupils the opportunity to view the world from different standpoints, helping them to question prejudice and develop open mindedness. Teachers have a major role to play in preparing young people for adult life; this means life in a multicultural multilingual Europe which in its turn is interdependent with the rest of the world. (NCC, 1990b)

Further NCC newsletters and circulars in the following year affirmed these points of view by maintaining that multicultural education broadened the pupils' horizons so that they could understand and contribute to a pluralist society; and that the variety of languages that one could encounter provided an opportunity to gain first-hand experiences of other cultures. In some Haringey junior schools, language surveys have

revealed that as many as twenty-eight different languages are spoken – this is a ric
resource which our schools use.

There is a variety of material from which one can construct an approach or polic
towards multicultural education. However, as Her Majesty's Inspectorate (HM
Annual Report on Education in England 1990–1991, of January 1992 observed, 'Mo
institutions have policies for promoting equality of opportunity but too often the ga
between policy and practice is unacceptably wide' (HMI 1992).

The Office for Standards in Education (OFSTED) produces the *Handbook for tf
Inspection of Schools*. The section on equal opportunities states that schools ar
evaluated by the extent to which 'all pupils, irrespective of gender, ability (includin
giftedness), ethnicity and social circumstance, have access to the curriculum and mak
the greatest progress possible' (OFSTED, 1993). The specific evidence that should b
looked at is itemized in the handbook, and the report on the school should include a
evaluation of 'the school's policy for equality of opportunity and the effects on th
quality of learning and standards of achievement; how well the policy is understooc
implemented and monitored in terms of opportunities and support arrangements fc
individuals and different groups'. Many teachers are aware of the gaps that can b
found between the intentions of a broad and balanced curriculum, what is actuall
offered, and what is received or positively taken up by each individual pupil.

As an LEA we have policy statements regarding equal opportunities, and ou
schools will have their policy statements that usually endorse and go on to furthe
explain this. These statements have been refined to include practical guidelines for th
whole school on, for example: staffing and organization, arrangements for parent:
behaviour and conduct not only in class but also in playgrounds and corridors. Subjec
and perspective inspectors, Inset co-ordinators and classroom practitioners are awar
of the need when planning the curriculum to include this multicultural theme into th
programmes of study, their teaching and learning strategies, their provision of learnin
resources, assessment and evaluation.

The guidelines will possibly include indicators of good practice, for example:

- word-processing software in the variety of languages which the pupils speak
  worksheets, manuals that show a range of women and men from a variety of ethni
  and multicultural backgrounds engaged in information technology activities;
- creating a database about festivals, foods and other class information that enable
  information technology capability in social, cultural and historical contexts in othe
  subjects.

Indicators of good practice come from our own authority schools, reports from HM)
research bodies, the National Council for Educational Technology (NCET), and othe
national bodies and agencies. Teachers respect the cultural background of ethni
minority pupils by:

- valuing their cultures by drawing on their knowledge and experience in the learnin
  process;
- acknowledging their competence in different languages and dialects;
- offering positive images and role models from all cultures.

It is important not to see multicultural education as a 'subject', but as a dimensio
which permeates the entire curriculum. As such, it should be at the heart of curriculum

planning, development and implementation. In *Curriculum Guidance 8: Education for Citizenship* (NCC, 1990a), objectives include promoting respect for different ways of life, beliefs, opinions and ideas, and providing the opportunity to discuss differences and resolve conflict. These objectives are expanded in one of the eight essential components, 'A Pluralist Society'. Possible areas of study in this are:

- the interdependence of individuals, groups and communities;
- similarities and differences between individuals, groups and communities and their effects;
- the existence of differences in perception and the ways in which these may be reconciled;
- Britain as a society made up of many cultures, ethnic groups, faiths and languages;
- the diversity of cultures in other societies;
- a study of human development and culture from different perspectives;
- international and global issues;
- the origins and effects of racial prejudice in British and other societies.

The statutory orders for foundation subjects published so far present opportunities to incorporate multicultural matters into teaching:

Design and Technology for ages 5 to 16: Proposals of the Secretary of State for Education and Science and the Secretary of State for Wales, June 1989:

Equal Opportunities
Ethnic Minorities
1.44 Cultural diversity has always been a feature of British life and there are positive advantages to be drawn from the different traditions represented in society. In schools, the different cultural and linguistic backgrounds of pupils are now becoming valued properly as a means of developing a richer learning environment for all.
1.45 However, the teaching of design and technology gives rise to problems which will require perception and sensitivity from teachers. Design and technology has its technical language, aspects of which may have no counterparts in the mother tongues of some young children in schools. Children from different ethnic backgrounds may bring to design and technological activities solutions which reflect different beliefs and practices, especially when food materials and environmental designs are involved. Indeed, the meaning and interpretation of design can vary in significant ways from culture to culture.
1.46 It is important that teachers take a positive approach to a mixed range of cultural backgrounds in their pupils, rather than an approach which concentrates on the problems that some pupils may have in coping with, for example, the language of design and technology. The variety of cultural backgrounds of pupils can broaden the insight they all have into the range of appropriate, alternative solutions to perceived problems. There are rich opportunities here to demonstrate that no one culture has a monopoly of achievements in design and technology. Appreciations of this kind could both contribute to better international understanding and yield direct economic benefits in later life. It is equally important that schools where there are few or no ethnic minority pupils ensure that their pupils understand the cultural diversity of modern society and are aware of the diversity existing in areas in which they may later live or work. Design and technology, like other subjects in the curriculum, has an important part to play in preparing pupils for life in a multi-cultural society. (DES, 1989d)

Science for ages 5 to 16: Proposals of the Secretary of State for Education and Science and the Secretary of State for Wales, August 1988:

Science and Cultural Diversity

7.12 Science education must take account of the ethnic and cultural diversity that the school population and society at large offers. Although the skills of observation, prediction, analysis and experimentation characterise the view of Science and science education which we have taken, we recognised that interpretation of the nature of Science may vary from culture to culture. It is in the implementation of the science curriculum that account needs to be taken of the special needs of ethnic minority children.

7.13 It is self-evident that a child who has difficulties with the language of instruction will experience problems of communication which may affect her or his receptiveness to Science and other areas of the curriculum. The language of Science can be complex, and the science teacher will naturally seek to be sensitive to the children's understanding of language and especially terminology when introducing scientific ideas and concepts. At the same time, the science teacher, perhaps in consultation with a language specialist, can provide a range of tangible examples which will help children with language problems to widen their vocabulary and powers of communication through their science lessons – for example, through carefully structured group discussion linked to planning and reporting practical activities.

7.14 The TGAT (Task Group on Assessment and Testing) report referred to the 'halo' effect where, in the absence of a close definition of what to look for in performance, we seek to confirm our expectations. Like everyone else, ethnic minority pupils will respond to others' expectations of them. It is important, then, that in designing learning activities and assessment tasks, care should be taken to avoid any ethnic and/or cultural bias.

7.15 It is well established that the choice of context in Science has a strong effect on a pupil's performance, and this applies particularly to ethnic minority pupils. It is important that the pupils' own experiences should be used as a basis for learning so that they can genuinely be agents of that learning. Science readily lends itself to the use of different social contexts, for example, in relation to diet, nutrition, energy, health, the ecosystem, and cultural diversity could thus help to enrich the quality of science education for all pupils provided the teacher does not adopt a narrow view of 'correctness' – for example in a discussion about diet or alternative technologies.

7.16 More generally, the science curriculum must provide opportunities to help all pupils recognise that no one culture has a monopoly of scientific achievement – for example, through discussion of the origins and growth of chemistry from ancient Egypt and Greece to Islamic, Byzantine and European cultures, and parallel developments in China and India. It is important, therefore, that science books and other learning material should include examples of people from ethnic minority groups working alongside others and achieving success in scientific work. Pupils should come to realise that the international currency of Science is an important force for overcoming racial prejudice.

7.17 We have drawn up our proposals in a flexible structure designed to encourage individual pupils to strive to reach the highest levels of which they are capable within a common set of curricular objectives. We believe that such a structure, which should develop a sense of confidence amongst all the pupils, is thereby best designed to serve the educational interests of ethnic minority pupils and prepare them for adult life and work. It is essential that this curriculum be interpreted in a way that is sensitive to the special needs of individual pupils of different cultural and linguistic backgrounds and cultural diversity of modern English and Welsh society. (DES, 1988d)

Mathematics for ages 5 to 16: **Proposals of the Secretary of State for Education and Science and the Secretary of State for Wales, August 1988:**

Ethnic and Cultural Diversity
10.18 Children whose mother tongue is not English are clearly likely to be at a disadvantage when they start school, compared with fluent English speakers. They may also be disoriented by differences between their home culture and the culture of the school. A further problem may be overt or covert racial prejudice: some teachers may unconsciously have lower expectations of pupils from certain ethnic minority backgrounds.

10.19 It is outside our remit to address the language problems of children for whom English is a second language. Clearly language difficulties can severely inhibit a child's capacity to learn in all subjects, not excluding mathematics. Local education authorities make special provision to help children in this position; for example, through appointment of bilingual instructors and through the laying on of special language classes.

10.20 It is sometimes suggested that the multi-cultural complexion of society demands a 'multi-cultural' approach to mathematics, with children being introduced to different number systems, foreign currencies and non-European measuring and counting devices. We are concerned that undue emphasis on multi-cultural mathematics, in these terms, could confuse young children. Whilst it is right to make clear to children that mathematics is the product of a diversity of cultures, priority must be given to ensuring that they have the knowledge, understanding and skills which they will need for adult life and employment in Britain in the twenty-first century. We believe that most ethnic minority parents would share this view. We have not therefore included any 'multi-cultural' aspects in any of our attainment targets.

10.21 However it will be important for teachers, within the broad framework of National Curriculum attainment targets and programmes of study, to select examples and materials which relate to the cultural backgrounds of their pupils. It may help if teachers, in planning lessons, can use contexts or material drawn from the backgrounds of their pupils. Some attention to the history of mathematics could show the contribution to the development of mathematical thinking of non-European cultures; for example, it would be right to point out that the number system is of Hindu-Arabic origin.

10.22 Many of those who argue for a multi-cultural approach to the mathematics curriculum do so on the basis that such an approach is necessary to raise the self-esteem of ethnic minority cultures and to improve mutual understanding and respect between races. We believe that this attitude is misconceived and patronising. Pupils with language problems will certainly need extra help. It is also important that knowledge and understanding of mathematics is not held back by any teaching methods or forms of school organisation which inadvertently discriminate against minority groups.

10.23 The ways in which pupils from different ethnic backgrounds are assessed will of course need to take these factors into account if the assessment is to give a true indication of the child's capabilities. For example, there will need to be provision for adapting SATS so that they are set in contexts with which pupils are familiar. Pupils with a poor command of English may need to be tested in their mother tongue if their mathematical attainment is to be fairly assessed. However, the key principle is that the attainment targets and programmes of study are the same for all pupils regardless of race. (DES, 1988c)

English for ages 5 to 11: Proposals of the Secretary of State for Education and Science and the Secretary of State for Wales, November 1988:

Equal Opportunities
Introduction
11.1 . . . it further notes that the curriculum should take account of 'the ethnic diversity of the school population and society at large', and draws attention to the principle that as wide a range of children as possible should have access to the whole curriculum.

11.2 Issues of equal opportunity may arise in a number of contexts, for example, those of gender, race, disability and religion. Such issues must be a concern of those devising the National Curriculum because the attainment targets and programmes of study must not be biased, deliberately or unwittingly, towards or against any such group. In particular, the National Curriculum assessment methods must enable all pupils to demonstrate what they can do, without the assessment of their performance being unfairly affected by the context of the task or the preconceptions of the assessor.

11.5 It is beyond our brief to attempt a general statement about equal opportunities in education. There are however, certain aspects which have particular importance in English teaching. It is through people's use of language that judgments are often made about their background, abilities and intelligence; and it is through literature and other language media that culture is itself expressed.

The content of the curriculum

11.6 English teachers need to be ready to give careful introductions and support when using texts which might otherwise cause offence to some groups, for example if a character with racist attitudes is portrayed, even though the author may not be supporting such attitudes. The choice of subjects for imaginative writing may also require care.
11.7 We discuss in chapter 7 the criteria for a balanced selection of literature in the classroom: it should include both British and non-British, both female and male authors, etc. The books chosen for study should also encompass a balanced range of presentations of other societies, and of ethnic and social groupings and life-styles within our own society.

Tasks and assessment

11.9 Children should be judged on what they can do and on what they know, not on who they are. But to ignore the evidence of differences in performance between gender or ethnic groups can lead to unjust treatment of individuals.
11.10 Substantial research has shown that different ethnic groups (e.g. children of Caribbean or Asian origin) display different ranges of attainments in the British education system. There are also documented differences between the average test performances of girls and boys in different curricular subjects. And a strong association between social background and educational attainment is one of the best demonstrated findings of educational research. The causes of such differences are not well understood. But curricular and assessment arrangements should aim to raise expectations and to help to narrow the gap wherever possible.
11.11 As well as such differences in educational attainment, there are differences in the characteristic linguistic behaviour of various groups. It is here also that English teachers have particular responsibilities. The possibility of bias arises especially in the assessment of oracy, because of the difficulty of separating pupils' spoken language from perceptions of their personality and background.
11.13 Language behaviour is influenced not only by personality but also by convention and culture. Speakers of different languages and cultural backgrounds, and from different social groups, vary quite significantly in their preferred language norms. There is a growing body of research which shows that cultures differ in the way conversations and other forms of spoken discourse are conducted. Features of interaction such as body posture, gesture, preferred distance between speakers, discursive styles, the ways in which politeness is marked or attention to other speakers signalled, differ widely across cultures. Other research illustrates the kinds of cross-cultural communication problems which can arise in interviews and other institutional settings.

Conclusions

11.16 Throughout the English curriculum and in the assessment process, teachers should enable all pupils, regardless of gender, ethnic or social groups, first to reflect on their performance, and then actively to seek to adapt their language characteristics to situation and purpose. (DES, 1988b)

In 1992 the National Union of Teachers produced a leaflet of curriculum guidelines to aid the teacher in finding opportunities for 'permeation' of the various core and foundation subjects with multicultural and anti-racist approaches (NUT, 1992). This was produced because thus far the National Curriculum Council had not issued guidance to support teachers in implementing these twin aims. Its guidelines were as follows, and include much pragmatic curricular advice:

Art (DES, 1992a)

The general statutory requirements for all Key Stages indicate that pupils should understand and appreciate art in varied genres and styles from a variety of cultures, Western and non-Western. Pupils should, for example, learn about influences from African art on Western artists.

Art displayed in school should therefore come from a wide range of cultures and periods, and displays should stimulate interest in artefacts, designs and pictures from many different parts of the world. A sense of excitement about the possibilities of the art curriculum for exploring different genres and media, and the pleasure in the activity of pupils creating for themselves varied forms through art, craft and design, should be fostered. Through these activities, pupils should learn about the interaction of different artistic traditions at different times and in different parts of the world. They should be given a sense of the intrinsic value of art produced by the whole range of cultural traditions worldwide, so they are not led to believe Western art is superior to that of other cultural traditions. The statutory orders will not contain lists of approved artists for study, so there is an infinite variety of choice possible. It would be of value for practising artists who visit schools to work with pupils who come from a range of different cultural backgrounds and artistic traditions.

Key Stage 3 programme of study for art says pupils should 'recognise the diverse ways that artists working in different cultures view and represent the world'. In examples, mention is made of how pupils could learn to recognize and value representations of similar forms in different cultures, e.g. the kite in Chinese, Japanese. For Indian and European traditions, examples of different uses of letters and symbols are given as Egyptian hieroglyphics, Islamic calligraphy and Chinese characters. Teachers may find the work of the 'Arts Education in a Multicultural Society' project useful. Visits to exhibitions of non-Western art, as well as those of local and indigenous artists, the Commonwealth Institute, parts of the Victoria & Albert Museum and the British Museum, as well as galleries containing European art, will stimulate interest in the infinite variety of styles and forms which pupils can be encouraged to emulate in their own work. This sense of excitement from visual stimuli should be encouraged from the very early years of education. The enjoyment children obtain from this subject can be of much value in establishing a truly multicultural dimension to the curriculum where a range of artistic traditions are valued, and it is to be hoped that art education does not suffer from becoming 'optional' at 14.

English (DES, 1988b)

Developing pupils' language skills, both oral and written, and the activity of learning to read for enjoyment and information, form the heart of the English curriculum.

The NCC Working Group report on English pointed out how important it is to build on pupils own linguistic experiences and skills, and to recognize bilingualism as a strength in language learning. Pupils should feel their own home languages are given value and status in the school; when support is given to pupils who are learning English as a second language, there should be just as high a level of teacher expectation of those pupils' eventual achievement as of all other pupils.

In the choice of reading books and literature to be studied, care should be taken to include black writers, and material should be drawn from a range of cultures and be appropriate to the ages of the pupils. For example, fairy tales, myths and legends from all around the world can be used to show the common experiences, hopes and fears of people in different cultures; the many black writers in English can widen horizons and relate experiences with which young black students can particularly identify and with which other students can empathize. Concerns have been expressed about the approved reading lists for reading test material. These will change over time, and teachers should not be unduly influenced by them in their selection of appropriate reading material which is relevant to their pupils' interests and can enlarge their understanding of other people's experience.

Recognition should also be given to the variety of accents, dialects and registers of spoken and written English in teaching about language use. It will be helpful to invite into school poets, storytellers and other writers to work with children, from a range of diverse ethnic and cultural backgrounds. This would need careful preparation, particularly in 'all white' schools, so that it does not become an 'exotic' feature, but is part of a planned programme. Schools could 'cluster' to share costs. Books chosen for school use should be checked for racist and sexist language and assumptions, and the school policy should be clear on how this matter is dealt with, to ensure a common approach. All these strategies should be set firmly in the context of an anti-racist approach, so that if adverse reactions are expressed by pupils, parents or governors they can be explained by the school's policy on educating against prejudice and racism.

English is probably the subject which has most scope for encouraging open discussion about attitudes and feelings towards racism; it can certainly be used to encourage pupils to detect bias and challenge stereotypes. Media education and drama can both be excellent vehicles for exploring questions of prejudice, bias and racism.

Space should be given to pupils to explore their own views, both orally and in writing, and pupils should be encouraged to respect differences of view while questioning unthinking prejudice. High standards of written and oral presentation should be expected of all pupils, and measures should be taken to reduce problems faced by second-language learners in the assessment process so that they are enabled to demonstrate their level of conceptual development. Inevitably this will not be easy in the early stages, but the children concerned should be given every encouragement to show their achievements so that their sense of self-worth is maintained.

Geography (DES, 1991a)

The geography syllabus appears at first sight to be overloaded with requirements for knowledge about the UK and European countries. However, there will be topics which could be chosen for early mapping work in physical geography on the local area which will raise issues about patterns of settlement, where people come from, and the sort of work they do, which will relate to patterns of migration and movement of families. Teachers can also use maps from different perspectives, for example, the Peters projection.

The programmes of study for 'knowledge and understanding of places' provide the opportunity for study of similarities and differences between the local area or home region and other localities, including 'economically developing' countries. Environmental aspects are covered, as well as reasons for disparities in wealth and the effects of international trade, including how the balance of trade may benefit some countries and disadvantage others.

The human geography attainment targets on population movements, settlements, journeys and communications give ample scope for introducing material about patterns of migration and the economic reasons for these. Environmental geography calls for pupils to 'explain the implications for international cooperation of resource and environment management' and to 'examine critically the concepts of sustainable development, stewardship and conservation'. Lessons about interdependence of peoples and countries, and the effects of international trade on economic development, will provide opportunities of teaching from an anti-racist perspective, and for enabling pupils to become aware of different values and interests in different parts of the world.

Teachers can draw on the experiences of pupils and their families to enrich understanding of aspects of geography and make it more relevant to students. In this context they should be aware that out-of-date textbooks sometimes contain offensive stereotypes and incorrect assumptions, which should be challenged.

History (DES, 1991b)

The history curriculum as set out in its attainment targets and programmes of study is quite tightly defined and centres around specific study units at each key stage, with a strong emphasis on British and European history. Nevertheless, there are opportunities within the units to teach from an anti-racist and multicultural perspective.

For example, the study for Key Stage 1 offers pupils opportunities to investigate changes in their own lives and those of their family or adults around them, which gives the occasion to draw on immediate memories from the locality in all its diversity. Awareness of the past can be developed through progressing from familiar situations to those more distant in time and place, and famous men and women and events from many different countries and cultures could be studied. Though the Statutory Core Study Units at the other key stages have a predominantly British and European focus (Romans, Anglo-Saxons, Vikings, Tudors and Stuarts, Victorian Britain, etc.), Ancient Greece and 'Explorations and Encounters 1450–1550' are also included.

At Key Stage 3, 'The Making of the United Kingdom: Crowns, Parliaments and Peoples 1500–1750' and 'Expansion, Trade and Industry Britain 1750–1900' could both include accounts of the contribution of people from all parts of the world to these developments. Pupils are asked to 'identify differences in the ways in which past events have been interpreted, for example: different views about the expansion of the British Empire in the late nineteenth century' and 'to develop an understanding that interpretation of the past can be conveyed in different ways through different media, for example: the different ways in which films, pictures and written accounts convey views about North American Indians in the nineteenth century'. These are actual examples given in NCC documents. What is most important is that in any such teaching it is not just the perspective of the British or European explorer that is given, but that of indigenous peoples in parts of the world to which Europeans travelled and in many cases exploited for their resources and labour. It should be pointed out that many parts of the world are still suffering the consequences of the colonial period, slavery, and the movements of people to work to produce wealth. Such themes can be developed by teachers in relation to the core units, and must be handled sensitively, depending on the interests and level of maturity of students.

At Key Stage 4 pupils are to be taught about concepts and terms necessary for an understanding of twentieth-century history, including: liberalism, conservatism, totalitarianism, socialism, capitalism, materialism, the welfare state, nationalism, imperialism, decolonization, conservation, equal opportunities, ecumenism, and in studying these themes 'pupils should have opportunities to develop awareness of how the histories of Britain, Europe and the world are linked'. There is plenty of opportunity here for teaching political literacy, a questioning approach, strategies for detection of bias, and analysis of different points of view. Throughout each key stage, teachers are advised to teach pupils about the 'Social, cultural, religious and ethnic diversity of the societies studied and the experiences of men and women in these societies'.

Key Stage 4 specifically requires teaching about how 'cultural, ethnic and religious differences within and between societies have influenced relations between communities and nations'. Although the syllabus keeps referring back to the importance of knowledge of British history, there is ample scope for widening horizons to include the rest of the world, and it would be a very narrow historian who did not take that view.

Mathematics (DES, 1988c)

Teachers will be familiar with the well-publicized controversy about 'multicultural mathematics' and the ill-judged comments on this subject by a former Prime Minister which had an unfortunate effect on subsequent developments.

The NCC Working Group report on mathematics makes it clear that it is important for teachers to select examples and materials which relate to the cultural background of their pupils. Children need to know the history of the development of mathematics and the contribution made by non-European cultures to the subject. For example, the number system we use derives from Hindu and Arabic mathematics. Knowledge about the historical roots of mathematics can make the subject more interesting for all pupils. Since mathematics is a 'core' subject studied by everyone, and a subject with considerable value and status, it is a powerful medium for anti-racist and multicultural teaching. There are many examples from different cultures which can enrich the study of mathematics: for example, mathematical games from around the world can be used to improve skills. Mathematics teachers report that using this approach makes the subject more interesting and accessible to pupils and thereby raises achievement levels for all, not just those from ethnic minority groups.

The programmes of study, statements of attainment and examples used give scope for using many different activities which derive from a range of cultural backgrounds. In teaching about symmetry, for example, patterns from many different cultures (e.g. African, Asian and Latin American and Diwali patterns) may be used; or, for tessellation, Islamic patterns. Mathematics has many practical applications which can draw on pupils' daily lives and backgrounds, and should reflect diversity of experience. For pupils whose first language is not English, there will be many opportunities to excel in mathematical tasks which are often possible to offer non-verbally, and opportunities should arise from collaborative problem-solving, which can enhance language development. It will also be useful if early mathematics materials can be produced in some of the most commonly used community languages, so that mathematical language does not inhibit mathematical development. Bilingual 'dictionaries' of common mathematical terms can be a helpful aid.

Modern Foreign Languages (DES, 1992a)

In response to representations, the statutory orders for modern foreign languages list alphabetically a selection of modern languages which may be taken as foundation subjects at Key Stages 3 and 4. (These are the following: Arabic, Bengali, Chinese (Cantonese or Mandarin), Danish, Dutch, French, German, Greek (Modern), Gujarati, Hebrew (Modern), Hindi, Italian, Japanese, Punjabi, Portuguese, Russian, Spanish, Turkish, Urdu.) This gives schools the opportunity to review their policy on modern language teaching, and to offer alternative modern languages to the most commonly taught European languages, where they can find teachers and where pupils and parents would like alternatives.

The logistical difficulties are considerable in terms of finding trained teachers and developing resources, particularly under LMS, but decisions made convey important messages about the status and value given by the school to non-European languages. It is, however, important to note that a non-European language only counts as a foundation subject where an EC language is also on offer in the school. It should not be assumed that pupils from ethnic minority backgrounds will necessarily choose to study a language spoken at home, though they may welcome this opportunity. Equally, if a language such as Urdu or Gujarati is offered, it should be open to all pupils and afforded equal status through timetabling arrangements.

The choice of languages taught can also widen horizons about other cultures and civilizations for pupils, and to study even one foreign language, and to learn about the country where it is spoken, and its literature, can generate curiosity and willingness to learn about other societies. Modern language learning is therefore an important tool in multicultural and anti-racist education. Although the National Curriculum only requires one modern foreign language to be studied, pupils should have the opportunity to follow courses in more than one should they so wish. Pupils should learn about the different forms of the language studied and spoken by different groups of people in different parts of the world; for example, French is used in some West African countries and parts of the Caribbean, Spanish and Portuguese in South America, Dutch in Indonesia, stemming from the colonial period.

School language policies should be sensitive to the varieties of languages already spoken in the school, and every effort should be made to give status to bilingualism or multilingualism as an achievement which is actually the norm in many other parts of the world.

The economic usefulness of other languages should also be stressed. Schools should make every effort to offer non-statutory languages as part of the curriculum, if possible to GCSE and A level, and to offer facilities for community language classes which pupils and adults may share, thus building links with the wider community.

Music (DES, 1992b)

Pupils should have the opportunity to listen to and learn to appreciate music from a wide variety of cultural traditions. As the report of the Music Working Group states: 'All pupils' lives are enriched by an understanding of their own cultural heritage, and by seeing that heritage valued in society.' We believe that schools should therefore reflect in their choice of music not only the varied cultural backgrounds of their pupils, but also a wide range of those cultures not represented in their school. Music is an activity in which all pupils can share, both in practical music-making and in appreciation.

In learning about the common features as well as differences in music from different cultures, pupils can have very positive experiences of different musical forms which can give cohesion to the musical education offered in school. As the Music Working Group says, it is important to ensure that different kinds of music retain their cultural·and stylistic integrity and are experienced by all pupils, yet to understand that the meeting of cultures can produce legitimate musical fusion. The Working Group recommends being sensitive to cultural sensibilities in introducing certain activities (e.g., pop music and dance), and points out usefully that some cultures introduce pupils to singing at a later stage than others. It also suggests bringing into school the musical experience and skills present in the community, musicians from different cultural and musical traditions should be invited into school to work with pupils.

The Secretaries of State expressed the belief that pupils from African, Caribbean and Asian backgrounds should be taught about the Western musical tradition in schools; we believe it is also important for white English and Welsh pupils to learn about music from other cultural traditions so that they do not gain a false impression of the 'superiority' of the so-called Western classical composers. It is likely that the choice of repertoire will be left to the professional discretion of teachers, so there is plenty of opportunity to give value to a variety of musical traditions. Teachers can draw on specialist professional help through Regional Arts and Music Centres, Community Arts organizations and Afro-Caribbean and Asian music, dance and theatre groups.

Physical Education (DES, 1992c)

All children should be able to participate in a wide range of physical education activities, regardless of ethnic background. There should be no assumption that specific activities are more attractive to one ethnic group than another, or that pupils from African and Caribbean backgrounds will automatically excel at sport rather than in intellectual activities.

Nevertheless, the success of black athletes can be drawn upon in terms of offering positive role models for all young people, and games which encourage co-operation and interaction between pupils of different ethnic groups can help break down prejudices and increase bonds of friendship and co-operation across cultural groupings.

Attention needs to be paid to dress requirements for various PE activities, including swimming and dance, to ensure that no cultural and religious groups are excluded. All these activities, and especially movement and dance for both boys and girls, offer pleasurable ways of exploring issues to do with personal identity, challenging racism, prejudice and stereotypes. Teachers should draw on games and dance from a variety of cultures. There needs to be more information on this possible range of activities available in teacher education. The Union welcomed the Working Group report on physical education, and especially its section on equal opportunities, which was very forward-looking and could be influential in securing changed approaches to the subject if backed up by initial and in-service training for teachers.

Religious Education

Religious education is part of the basic curriculum for each school, and although it is not subject to the same nationally prescribed arrangements as National Curriculum subjects, it must be taught in accordance with an agreed syllabus drawn up at local level by the Standing Advisory Council on Religious Education (SACRE) for each LEA.

There have been very many successful agreed syllabuses drawn up by SACREs, which reflect the cultural diversity of their areas. Since the 1988 Act, the syllabus must 'reflect the fact that the religious traditions in Great Britain are in the main Christian whilst taking account of the teaching and practices of the other principal religions represented in Great Britain'. In county schools the agreed syllabus is followed, whereas voluntary aided schools follow the school's own scheme agreed at diocesan level or in accordance with their trust deed. In the circular issued to explain the ERA's provisions in relation to RE, the statement is made that 'The Government believes that all those concerned with religious education should seek to ensure that it promotes respect, understanding and tolerance for those who adhere to different faiths.'

The NCC recognizes that each LEA determines its own RE syllabus according to local circumstances. It has not issued formal guidance on introducing attainment targets or programmes of study, but in a discussion paper, 'A Local Curriculum Framework' (1991), it suggests how these may be applied to RE if desired. It indicates two broad areas that pupils should cover – they should 'understand the teachings and practices of Christianity and other world religions' and 'be encouraged to develop their own beliefs and values'. DES ministers have emphasized the importance of RE in recognizing Britain's ethnic diversity and encouraging respect for different faiths within the school community. The Union would wish to add that it is most important that pupils' own beliefs are respected in school, and it must be recognized that many will come from homes which do not practise any religion.

Religious education has always offered possibilities for encouraging sensitivity to a variety of beliefs and practices. It also offers in each religion studied the opportunity for learning what the various faiths have to teach about opposition to racial prejudice and discrimination. It is important that pupils learn about each of the major world religions and its spiritual insights, and that they understand the part played by these religions in ordinary people's lives in all parts of the world. Studying what different religions have to say about moral values and respect for individuals will help pupils work out their own system of beliefs and moral codes, and should foster respect between the different religious traditions of pupils in the school.

Science (DES, 1988d)

Although one of the original targets concerned with the history of science has been removed in the revision of the Order, there is still reference in the overall programmes of study at Key Stages 3 and 4 to pupils' need to become familiar with the history of science, and this could include contributions from different parts of the world. There are useful accounts of the contributions made by black scientists to the development of science. It is also noteworthy that there are many research scientists from the Indian subcontinent and other parts of the world leading scientific research in Europe and the USA. Pupils need this awareness to combat the stereotype of science as the product of Western industrialized societies alone.

As in other subjects, the choice of topics for exploration in science can draw upon experiences in pupils' everyday lives and from a range of diverse cultural backgrounds. The language and specialized vocabulary of science needs to be made available to all pupils, especially those needing English language support. Often pupils from ethnic minority groups excel at science and find a sense of achievement from the practical activities offered by the subject. Care should be taken by teachers to avoid stereotyped expectations of achievement based on linguistic competence alone, and all pupils should be stretched and able to take the double science option at Key Stage 4 if they show ability in the subject (girls as well as boys).

Technology (DES, 1989d)

Development of technology skills should, especially in the early stages, be derived from and relevant to pupils' everyday experiences. The areas of study chosen can draw on common human activities between all societies, such as food production, and awareness of the origins of many types of food in different parts of the world can help break down prejudices. Other topics such as shelter and homes are excellent for teaching from an anti-racist perspective and for dispelling stereotypes as well as emphasizing common human needs which give rise to technological invention.

Another aspect of teaching in technology which can show differences in values and foster appreciation of different traditions is to ensure that pupils realize that a 'high technology' solution is not always appropriate, especially in developing countries, where interaction with cultural practices and economic factors is very important. Furthermore, pupils should learn that access to information technology can be empowering and is important for independent learning for students from all ethnic groups and both genders equally.

The advisory groups that made these recommendations garnered good practice and experience from within the classroom either directly or indirectly. They depended on input and continual monitoring and evaluation evidence from inspectors, advisers, headteachers and teachers. Whether it be demographically, pedagogically or philosophically, the classroom of tomorrow will not only be computerized, it will also be multicultural.

Chapter 5

Control Technology in the Primary Classroom

Grace Woodford

Twenty years ago computers were not part of the curriculum or the primary classroom. It would have been difficult to predict in 1970 what the classroom would look like twenty years thence. Some of the major changes that have taken place include the introduction of computers in the classroom, and the National Curriculum. It is equally difficult to predict what the curriculum or the classroom will look like in twenty years time. The computer has been accepted as a tool for learning, and the National Curriculum Information Technology document, with its five strands, sets out a clear progression through each of the levels.

My experience for the last ten years has been as an advisory teacher in primary science and technology, not as an information technology specialist. I have been involved with how the computer can be used to enhance learning in design technology and science with specific reference to measurement and control. During this period there has been a rapid growth in control technology and the use of sensors to capture data in science.

The contributing factors to this growth are:

- the Education Support Grant (ESG) scheme which provided funding for advisory teachers and resources information technology as well as science and technology;
- the in-service training given to classroom teachers;
- the framework of the National Curriculum documents;
- investigations in science;
- skills and knowledge to enable children to design and make models to control by using the computer;
- enormous commitment of primary teachers;
- manufacturers providing the hardware and the software at affordable prices.

The Development of Computer Control Technology in the Primary Classroom

In the early 1980s design technology was in its infancy in the primary classroom. At the same time, craft, design and technology (CDT) was developing in secondary schools in place of traditional woodwork and metalwork. There were a few enthusiasts in primary schools who were interested in 3-D working models. One of the limiting factors was the difficulty young children had in joining resistant materials. In the infant schools, junk modelling was accepted as good practice, and here children joined found materials with PVA glue.

Junior children encountered problems with joining materials when building structures. A method was tried in which strip wood was joined by drilling holes in wood and inserting dowel; however, this required a degree of accuracy which many children did not have. David Jinks (Williams and Jinks, 1985) pioneered the method of joining strip wood with glue and triangles, and this simple idea enabled primary design and technology to take a quantum leap! Children could now make geared motorized machines, and using the computer to control these was a natural progression. By this time computers were beginning to be an integral part of the curriculum. Advisory teachers provided, through the ESG scheme, INSET for teachers to give them the knowledge and skills in both design technology and computer control. There was also time to work alongside teachers in their classrooms.

Interface boxes such as the Deltronics box became available; this was a step forward from that of teachers making their own interface boxes on courses. The software became more user-friendly, language such as 'switch on' was used instead of using BASIC programming instructions.

Computer control involves using an interface box which is controlled by the computer and which when instructed switches lights, motors or buzzers on or off. Children can soon learn to write a program which will control a sequence such as traffic lights or disco lights. They can also learn how to switch a motor on in a forward direction or a backward direction. Problems arise when children want to use a motor to drive something without a geared system. Many primary teachers find the concept of gearing a difficult one, but when certain knowledge and skills are understood, then the possibilities for making machines that work in the primary classroom are increased. Children can make models that can be controlled with input switches; for instance, car park barrier which needs an input sensor to raise the barrier, an input sensor to stop the barrier when fully raised and another sensor to stop the barrier when lowered.

Recent Developments

The BBC computer was used with a Deltronics interface box, and various types of software were available, including Control It, Comtrol, and Contact. A more recent development includes using the Archimedes and Coco software, in which the voice function on the computer can be used and the mouse is used to make the writing of the program a shorter task.

Lego have introduced Control Lab, which has software for the Nimbus, the Apple Mac and the Archimedes. Diagrams on the screen are activated with the mouse (e.g.

to turn a switch on, the picture of the switch is clicked with the cursor into an 'on' position and the output switches on. Procedures and programs can also be written.

What Will the Future Bring?

A supposition for the future is that a more technological age will develop and the current exponential growth rate will reach a point when it will slow down. Could it be that we are now in the stage of exponential growth, and that the computer is the major breakthrough, and that from now on we will see refinements in terms of size and capacity and quantity?

Control technology will still be about children making their own models to control with a computer. Construction kits such as Lego Dacta and Fischer Technic help at the modelling stage, and manufacturers are aware of the potential for this type of product and will bring more attractive educational sets to the market. The technical problems of making a successful model will be similar, but improvements could be made by the development of new glues which would be faster to set. The most significant improvement would be a super elastic band, then problems of finding the right size and of them rotting would be eliminated.

The National Curriculum in whatever form it takes will, one hopes, set out a progression in skills and knowledge which will have been experienced by a whole new generation of people and thus be as much part of school as maths is today.

Lap-top computers will follow the path of the calculator and become an everyday item. These would be used to control much smaller interface boxes. Software has become simpler to use and yet the possibilities have become more complex. This trend would have to continue, maybe the voice-activated control package would be available by the year 2014!

Computers and Science in Primary Schools

Twenty years ago science in the primary classroom was, for most teachers, limited to the nature table and a study of seasonal events such as growing seeds, the tadpole, the caterpillar life cycle, and, in the autumn, seeds and fruits. Physical science and chemistry was more of a rarity. The Nuffield Junior Science scheme[1], published in 1967, helped to promote science in the primary school. This scheme was followed by the Schools Science 5 to 13[2] scheme in 1972, which gave a breadth to science teaching that had not hitherto been common practice. The scheme set out activities in a form which was accessible to primary teachers, and so science gradually became a subject area in the primary curriculum. In the early 1980s the APU carried out practical testing of children's understanding of science and discovered the areas of physical science which were most problematic to primary teachers. Since this time, science has become part of the curriculum and with the advent of the National Curriculum has to be taught by all primary teachers.

Computers and Primary Science Under the National Curriculum

The National Curriculum stresses the importance of children carrying out their own investigations in science. Children are required to:

- hypothesize, make predictions or test ideas;
- devise a fair test;
- quantify by measuring using appropriate instruments;
- collect data and record their results in a meaningful way;
- draw conclusions which link patterns in observation or results to the original question, prediction or idea.

Children can use data capture instruments to facilitate these investigative skills requiring accurate measurement. Primary children most commonly need to measure temperature, time and speed. Data capture software often records the data and has an integral graphing facility.

An example of the use of data capture in the primary classroom is illustrated in the case study on page 41 (see figure 5.1).

Computers Can Support the Teaching of Science in Other Ways

Communicating Information: Reports can be written using word-processing facilities.
Handling Information: Databases can be used to research information, there are programs such as Key Plus which contain information that can be interrogated. Children can make their own keys with programs such as Branch or Sorting Game. CD-ROMs can be used in an encyclopaedia format to find out information about scientific discovery or the habitats or life cycle of a given creature.
Measurement and Control (see figure 5.2): Children can record data over both long and short periods of time using data capture interface boxes such as Leicester Toolkit, Philip Harris First Sense and Sense It. There are remote data loggers such as Logit and Sense and Control which can be taken to a habitat for environmental work. This method of recording data has the advantage of graphing the results with time.
Modelling: Simulation programs can help with the understanding of scientific concepts (e.g., the Electricity Council produce Wattville, which simulates power in the home and in a town, and Power Control, which simulates power station operations; Suburban Fox and Pondlife are programs which model environments).
Application and Effects: Children have a number of opportunities to reflect on comparative use of information technology and traditional methods of collecting data.

Computers are being used in many primary classrooms; the question is, What will the classroom look like in twenty years time? We can envisage a new generation of teachers who use computers in much the same way as we use a calculator to aid calculations today.

NOTES

1. Nuffield Junior Science Scheme. Collins, 1967.
2. The School Science Scheme. 1972.

The children were engaged in a topic on materials. Their task was to devise a fair test to see which material was the best for keeping liquid warm in a bottle.

The children worked in groups of three, each choosing a material to wrap around the bottle. Only one group at a time worked on the activity because the computer was needed to monitor temperature changes over a period of time. This took most of the lesson. The classroom was organized with different tables of children doing different activities, some doing Maths, some Art, some English, and some working on the fair test. All would have a turn at the fair test during the course of the week.

The children had three identical bottles which they wrapped with different materials (e.g. hessian, wool and foil). They put equal measured amounts of hot water in each bottle and put a temperature probe in each. The probes were connected to the Leicester Box, and the Leicester Toolkit Software was used. The bottles were then left and the temperature was plotted against time.

A graph from the three different probes was drawn on the screen and then printed. The children could then repeat the exercise with different materials and make comparisons.

The advantages of using data logging as opposed to just thermometers and a stop-clock were that:

- synchronizing the readings with time was not necessary;
- the three temperatures were plotted and the graph drawn simultaneously;
- the display on the screen is clear and the relative temperatures are visually apparent;
- comparisons can be made by using the graph and drawing conclusions;
- the test can be repeated easily using other materials as insulators.

Figure 5.1   *Case study in the use of temperature probes with primary children: which material makes the best insulator?*

PROGRAMMES OF STUDY	STATEMENTS OF ATTAINMENT	SOFTWARE
Pupils should be taught:	Pupils should:	Software and/or devices that could be used:
KS1 • that control is integral in many everyday products	**1 b** • be able to talk about ways in which equipment, such as toys and domestic appliances, respond to signals or commands	**Programmable robots:** KS1/2 ROAMER PIP VALIANT FLOOR TURTLE
KS1 • how to give instructions to electronic devices	**3 b** • be able to give a sequence of direct instructions to control movement	**BBC Programs:**
L1 • to control everyday items and describe the effect of their actions		KS1/2 DART LOGO JUMBO (infant & 1st schools disc)
KS2 • to know that programmable devices can be controlled using sequences of instructions	**4 b** • be able to develop a set of commands to control the movement of a screen image or a robot; understand that a computer program or procedure is a set of instructions to be followed in a pre-determined sequence	KS2 CONTROL - IT CONTROL LOGO **ARCHIMEDES** KS1/2 DART PLUS
L5 • know that the order in which instructions are presented, and the form in which they are given to a computer, is important	**5 b** • understand that a computer can control devices by a series of commands, and appreciate the need for precision in framing commands.	
L5 • to write a simple computer program for a particular purpose		

NON-STATUTORY GUIDANCE

KS1

Pupils should investigate devices which use control mechanisms and discuss why control is needed. Programmable toys a:
everyday items such as automatic washing machines, microwave cookers, tape and video recorders are suitable for study. By t
end of the key stage pupils should be able to control such devices confidently and be able to give and follow simple sequences
instructions.

KS2

Pupils will devise and modify sets of instructions using a turtle graphics program or a programmable robot, and give reasons :
the order of their instructions. Some pupils will progress to using information technology to control models such as lev
crossing barriers and traffic lights.

Figure 5.2   *Information technology capability, Key Stages 1 and 2: measurement and control (DES, 1990b)*

Chapter 6

Learning Discovery Systems in the Computerized Classroom

Jon Griffin

Introduction

> Just a few years ago people thought of computers as expensive and exotic devices. Their commercial and industrial uses affected ordinary people, but hardly anyone expected computers to become part of day-to-day life. This view has changed dramatically and rapidly as the public has come to accept the reality of the personal computer . . . The appearance of the first rather primitive machines in this class was enough to catch the imagination of journalists and produce a rush of speculative articles about life in the computer-rich world to come . . . Most writers emphasised using computers for games . . . A few talked about the computer as a teaching machine.
> (Papert, 1982, p. 3)

Papert's and my interest is in how computers affect the way that people think and learn. It is his, and my, belief that computer systems can be developed so that learning can take place as a natural process. The analogy that he gives is that learning with a computer should be like learning French by living in France rather than by the unnatural process of learning it in a classroom (Papert, 1982, p. 6). It was also his belief that learning with a computer affects the way that other learning takes place. As a result of these beliefs he created logo – a computer language that is designed to allow discovery learning in a natural way in our classrooms.

In designing logo, Papert had at the back of his mind an image of the child as an epistemologist, and he was impressed by Piaget's view that children are active builders of their own intellectual structures. His thinking is that the notion

> that intellectual structures are built by the learner rather than taught by a teacher does not mean that they are built from nothing. On the contrary: Like other builders, children appropriate to their own use materials they find about them, most saliently the models and metaphors suggested by the surrounding culture.
> (Papert, 1982, p. 19)

So it is with logo. Children can experiment, find out and use their experiences and other clues to solve new problems. This thinking clearly fits in with Piaget's notions of Accommodation, Assimilation and Adaption' (McNally, 1974), and with my experience.

As a teacher educator, I am in primary schools regularly . This involves working wit student teachers, teachers, and pupils. In this chapter I aim to present two case studie to illustrate how the computer can affect the way that people learn and think, and t introduce the notion of 'Learning Discovery Systems in the Computerized Classroom' It is also my purpose to encourage educators to review their thinking about the way tha they use computers in the learning environment. In doing this we need to sto concentrating our thinking on the complexities of the computer, and instead focus o the learning that the computer engenders, including the learning that takes place awa from the computer. Indeed, the first of the two case studies looks at the learning tha takes in the pre-computer stage.

In the first case study I focused on pre-computer activities that relate to the sub theme 'Problem-solving and Control Technology in the Primary Classroom'. Thi project was carried out over a period of two terms and involved working with 4- and 5 year-old children from the reception class (although these activities were carried ou with 'Year R' children, they could easily be translated to other age groups). M teaching was serial, that is I taught in the school on only one day per week. This gav problems of continuity but meant that I had more time in which to reflect on activitie and prepare for the next week's work. The aim of this case study was to underline tha the experiences before and after the actual time spent at the computer are of extrem importance and should not be underestimated.

In the second case study, which was on the sub-theme of 'Logo Discovery Systems', compared the use of 'Logo Micro Worlds' with groups of children from a number o classes and covered the 4–11 age range. In carrying out this project I was able to addres issues such as continuity and progression, as well as addressing the notion of the spira curriculum. This project was carried out over a period of two weeks, and although i gave me less time to prepare and reflect on the teaching and learning that took place, i certainly enabled me to appreciate the problems that classroom teachers have t endure on a daily basis.

Both of these case studies support the theme of 'Learning Discovery Systems in th Computerized Classroom'. The main aim of this study was to look at compute technology, problem-solving, and discovery systems in the primary classroom, and i particular to work with younger children.

With the aid of parents and various grants, the school had enough computer system to provide one for each classroom. The children primarily used this technology fc activities such as word processing, information-handling, graphics and logo.

The children were mixed in their ability and provided an interesting challenge. The were always friendly, and generally responded to my attempts at teaching in a positiv manner. Thankfully, I was able to 'notch up' more successes than failures. On interesting and lovable girl was a 4-year-old called Hannah, who could only concen trate for about ten seconds at any one time. In assemblies she would stand up and loo round the hall, oblivious of what was going on around her – at least she did whenever did not have my camera to record the event!

Problem-Solving and Computers

'The primary school curriculum should be thought of in terms of activity and experience rather than knowledge to be acquired and facts to be stored' (Haddow, 1931). For its day, the Haddow report was forward-looking, and such thinking provides the basis for child-centred, discovery learning problem-solving activities. Despite efforts over the years to include such activities in the primary curriculum, many teachers prefer a didactic approach rather than reliance on discovery methods. It is not surprising, then, that teachers do not involve problem-solving activities in their teaching, as little is known about the ways in which these problem-solving processes develop, and suitable materials for children to use are not readily available. As a consequence of these shortcomings I realize that 'There is a need for more study of children's problem solving activities and the extent to which strategies for problem solving can be taught' (Cockcroft, 1982).

The introduction of the computer exacerbates the problem and encourages 'What if . . . ?' questions, as well as leading children naturally into investigations and problem-solving activities. Furthermore, the computer can help children to become confident and discriminating problem-solvers and users of information.

We as teachers should be aware of the potential of computer technology, and we should have the necessary insights, skills, strategies and confidence to use it effectively in our teaching. My interest in problem-solving stems from a practical background and career.

A problem I was once presented with was to build, for use by the public on an 'open day', a model of an aircraft which illustrated the principles of an automatic pilot. This problem, in its own way, was not very different from one tackled by a group of 8- and 9-year-old children in another primary school, who while doing a project on shopping became interested in the automatic doors at the local supermarket.

In order to further their understanding of how the doors worked, the children built a model which illustrated the principles by which the doors operated. This involved designing and making pressure pads to sense the customers approaching the doors, sensors to detect when the doors were fully open or fully closed, and then connecting the model to a computer for which they had written a computer program to control the sequence and operation of the doors. In doing this project the children discovered for themselves the principles involved, and in doing so their understanding of the relevant scientific phenomena was greatly enhanced. This learning came about in an environment which involved 'first-hand' experiences and one in which the children were in control of their own learning.

The parallels between the 'real-world' problem that I undertook and the 'classroom problem' that the children did are clear and important. All too often 'classroom problems' have no resemblance to the 'real world'.

I intend to concentrate on the sorts of problems that young children can tackle and which in some way are related to computer technology. These also include those problems which, although unrelated to computers and computer technology, could be extended into that area or will give children the problem-solving skills and strategies that they will require for tackling computer-based problems, particularly in control technology.

In the mid-1980s the Micro Electronics Primary Project produced a resource pack on 'problem solving and control technology' (MEP, 1985c). Within this pack are a number of simple problems which can be modified and which are ideal for children of all ages – they are well suited to infants. They also go some way to providing children with the skills and strategies that they require for problem-solving and for tackling more sophisticated problems. An added bonus is that teachers feel that the problems are at such a level that they can cope with them and manage the learning processes that the children go through with confidence. We can think of these problems as *starting-points* . . .

Problem-Solving and Control Technology in the Primary Classroom: A Case Study

The children started work on a number of problems which, including the three that follow, were based on problems to be found in the Micro Electronics Primary Project Pack.

The first was entitled 'Beef Thief'. For this problem, each pair of children was given a sheet of A4 card, three sheets of A4 paper, a beef oxo cube, sellotape and scissors (MEP, 1985).

One pair of children was asked to make towers as tall as they could which would support an oxo cube at the top. Another pair of children was asked to make their towers as short as they could; again, the towers had to support an oxo cube at the top. The children were given thirty minutes to solve this problem.

Alternative strategies might have involved the children being set the problem in such a way that they would have to build a structure which was of a specific height (e.g., 1 metre tall or 1.5 metres tall).

The first pair had no difficulty in getting started. They worked co-operatively and rapidly to produce a tower which used all of the paper and card. After some minor adjustments to the structure the tower supported the oxo cube.

The second pair, on the other hand, had great difficulty in getting started. Their problem was that they had too many resources and that as a result of their conditioning they were trying to use all of the paper and the card, and in doing this they knew that they would produce a tall structure. Once they were assured that they did not have to use all of the resources their task became relatively straightforward and they settled down to producing a short tower made out of one sheet of paper.

All children experienced some problems in cutting and using the sellotape effectively, and consequently there was some wastage of the sellotape. However, all of the children were delighted with their success. They were on the way to becoming adept problem-solvers . . .

Following this problem they tackled a similar activity to consolidate the skills and strategies that they had employed. This second activity involved the children in building a 'Channel Bridge' to span a gap of two metres between desks. The structure also had to support as much weight as possible at its centre. For this problem the children were given five sheets of A4 paper, sellotape, scissors and a metre rule (MEP, 1985c).

A selection of weights was used to test the strength of the bridge. The children worked in groups of three on this problem. The major problem to overcome was that, when laid end to end, the sheets of paper were not long enough to span the two-metre gap. The groups took between two and fifteen minutes to work out that the paper had to be cut – the norm being approximately five minutes.

One minor problem that was encountered was the use of sellotape. As a result of doing the 'Beef Thief' problem the children had improved their dexterity when using sellotape, but some of the children still needed help. All groups were successful in completing their bridges!

We had great fun testing their bridges, and the children were extremely keen to see how much their bridge would support before it gave way and broke. Prior to the bridges being tested to destruction, the children were asked where the weak points were. They were then given the opportunity to strengthen these weak points before the testing began. The bridges supported between approximately one and four kilograms: for most the breaking point was approximately two kilograms. The breaking point was a good indicator of how well the bridge had been built by the children, as they had used minor variations on one basic design. We were all pleased with the results, and everybody felt a great sense of achievement!

The third problem that the children tackled was used as an introduction to electrical circuits. The ability to construct a simple circuit is essential if children are to have success with the aspects of technology called 'Control Technology'. This problem was called the 'Big Switch'. It required the children to design, make and test a switch for turning a bulb on and off. They were given paperclips, drawing pins, kitchen foil, a strip of wood, a piece of strawboard, wire, a 4.5 volt battery, a 3.5 volt bulb and a bulb holder (MEP, 1985c).

The switch had to be easy to use with one hand and had to be sufficiently durable to last for three hundred switchings. Building the switch posed two major problems. The first was that of selection – which items the children should use. The second was how to connect the wire to the battery and bulb holder in order to make the bulb light – it was a picture to see the childrens' faces when they succeeded in lighting the bulb!

For this activity I had three pairs working at a time on the switch. On completion of the problem I got the children to draw a circuit diagram (with my assistance) – they found this to be a useful record of what they had done.

I was particularly struck by the similarity of a project undertaken by Kennedy (Kennedy and Robinson, 1991), in which the focus of his problems was art rather than information technology. In each of our studies we were keen to build on the childrens' understanding and experience by using the 'problems within problems' that the children encountered as they worked on the task-in-hand.

> A classroom where a range of activities are taking place and in which pupils express interests and ask questions can also provide on-the-spot problems. Teachers need to exploit these situations because there is greater motivation to solve problems which have been posed by the pupils themselves.
> (HMI, 1987)

In my activities I tried to exploit these on-the-spot problems.

Children are motivated when the problems are related to a theme or topic, and in this case I related the problems to the theme 'Little and Large'. Thus in the case of the 'Beef Thief' problem, the children made little and large towers, in the case of the 'Channel Bridge' problem small and large weights were used for testing, and in the case of the 'Big Switch' the switch had to operate a large number of times.

Sometimes it is necessary to set problems which in themselves do not relate directl
to the theme but which allow children to develop skills and strategies that are importar
to their development or which lead to the solution of problems that are related to th
theme being studied. Teachers should feel confident to include these problems whe
the need arises.

I have outlined three of the problems that the children tackled. What has not bee
mentioned is the art, computer usage (word processing with the aid of a concep
keyboard), language (both spoken and written), mathematics and science that cam
out of these and the other problems that the children tackled. This is not because I fee
that it is not important, but because of the need to concentrate on some starting-poin
for technology and problem-solving at this time. By reference to Kennedy's wor
(Kennedy and Robinson, 1991), it can be seen that the starting-points for this form o
problem-solving, with control technology as the end point, are similar to these for art.
am sure that these starting-points can also be used in other curricular contexts.

The effort and concentration that the children put into solving the problems wa
remarkable. Remember Hannah, who could normally not sit still or concentrate fc
more than a few moments at a time? She worked solidly on the 'Big Switch' problen
until it was finished (a little over an hour) – she even gave up her play-time because sh
was so engrossed and finishing was important. This was typical; indeed, it would mak
an interesting study in itself to investigate the effects of computer technology on th
concentration span of children, or its use as a motivator.

It is important to have some idea of how activities fit into the curriculum and wher
they are leading in terms of events to be experienced and concepts to be learned. Thu
it is essential to have a coherent plan. With the advent of the National Curriculum an
its stated aim that information technology should underpin it, we are getting close t
the point when such plans can fully emerge and children can build on prior experienc
and learning. In this case the activities are leading to a point in the future when th
children will be solving problems which have either been set for them by the teacher o
which they have set for themselves and which will involve some sort of control proce
which in turn may be controlled by a computer.

These problems might include:

- making and controlling a set of traffic lights or a model volcano;
- designing and making a clown's face which can be operated by batteries o
  controlled by a computer;
- designing and making a vehicle that can go forwards, backwards, left and right in
  given sequence;
- discovering how the local supermarket doors operate and then designing, makir
  and controlling a model which illustrates the principles involved.

There are of course a whole range of problem-solving activities involving compute
technology that I have not included in this study but which are equally appropriate fc
young children and are included within the National Curriculum.

I concentrated on three problems in order to outline one possible starting-point wit
young children for 'Problem-solving and Control Technology in the Primary Clas
room'. The work that I did in this school seems to have confirmed the notion tha
computer technology has an important part to play in the infant curriculum and tha
there are many activities within the scope of this age range. This work also reinforce

the notion that with computer technology what you do away from the computer is probably more important than what is done at the computer, and that the information technology should be an integral part of the curriculum.

Logo Discovery Systems: A Case Study

The second case study involving discovery systems which took place in this school was on the theme, 'Logo Discovery Systems'.

One of the problems with using microtechnology in the primary classroom is the lack of experience and tradition of using this technology. As a consequence there is a lack of continuity in the work being done in the classroom. This problem is exacerbated by the spiral curriculum. Teachers all too often do not consider the developmental stage that the children are at in this area and are often unaware of past experiences, which are very often limited, and they therefore find it difficult to start from a point which is familiar to the children. As the National Curriculum works its way through all four key stages this problem should disappear. We have all seen examples of the same computer program being used for the same educational purposes across the whole primary age range without giving children any opportunities for development and progression on each occasion that it was revisited.

Another aspect of computing that is often repeated throughout the primary school is Logo (Logotron, 1990). This is an area that interests me, and the purpose of this piece of research was to use the relevant literature and my experience to investigate the notion of curriculum continuity and formulate some strategies for tackling the spiral curriculum with regard to aspects of Logo (DES, 1990b, pp. B2, C10–13).

Logo is a computer language which owes its origins to Papert (an educationalist and mathematician at the Massachusetts Institute of Technology). The roots of Logo began in his early childhood with his fascination for cars and gears. He became adept at turning wheels in his mind and at making chains of cause and effect. Gears serving as models for mathematics carried abstract ideas into his mind. Much later, when he had read Piaget, his notion of using gears as a modelling tool seemed to fulfil Piaget's notion of assimilation (McNally, 1974). Papert then took Piaget's theories further (Papert, 1982).

One would therefore have expected that Papert's brainchild would have been a set of cogs and gears which students and pupils could use in some way for modelling and solving problems. His theory was, however, that what gears did for himself computers might do for others – hence the birth of Logo!

Logo is a very powerful language used for programming computers. For the purpose of my work in the school, I limited the work to the primitives forward, back, left and right. With these four instructions, by exploring microworlds of relevance and of interest to the children many problems can be solved, mathematical ideas investigated, discovered and learned, and a plethora of language work done. Due to the limited (non-existent) experience of the children that I worked with, we concentrated on exploring microworlds at a level appropriate to them. Hence the notion of the spiral curriculum and the need to look towards curriculum continuity for Logo in the future, when teachers will be in a position to build on past experiences.

For the purpose of this study I arranged to work with three groups of children. Group 1 was selected from a reception class, Group 2 from a Year Three class and Group 3 from a Year Six class. In all cases there were a wide range of abilities within each group and a balance between boys and girls. None of the children had any experience of Logo, and therefore all of the groups had to start from humble beginnings.

The first stage of this study started where the early exercises for all groups were aimed at getting the children to learn and be able to apply the primitives forward, back, left and right to new situations. Group 1 started with big trak,[1] while the other two groups started by role playing in pairs. The role play involved one of the pair being a robot and the other child being the controller. The child playing the controller had to give the other (the robot) precise instructions on how to move from one position to another specified position. This started off as a group activity.

The dialogue of Group 2 (Year Three children) was interesting. In this example Claire was giving Adam instructions:

> Claire   Right [slight pause] a bit more. Yes! that's it. Forward [pause] keep going [pause] STOP! [Adam stops] . . .

Then Alaina instructs Sarah:

> Alaina   Forward! Forward! Forward! [Richard takes one pace each time Alaina says, 'Forward'] Stop!

The next pair are Richard and Matthew. Richard does the instructing, and he clearly builds on what has gone before:

> Richard   Forward one, forward [short pause] three, right two [meaning turn right through two right angles] . . .

The children then worked happily in pairs and naturally moved into the symbolic stage (Bruner, 1982, p. 11) and derived their own lists of instructions that they gave to each other.

Group 3 (Year Six children) started off with the same exercise. They tackled this problem at a higher level and therefore got a lot more out of it. Their talk went as follows:

> Shvetal   . . . , right 80°.
>
> Andrew   No! you mean 180°.
> Shvetal   Yes, that's right, right 180°, forward 5, . . .

Group 3 then moved on to use Logo on the computer. This involved making up a game in which a young child (possibly their baby brother or sister) escapes from a playpen in the back garden. The problem was for the young child to visit the flower bed, greenhouse and pond in turn. Group 2 tackled a similar problem, which was related to their topic (flight and air).

I noted that as the children sat round the computer the boys sat at the front and the girls at the back. As a consequence the children were given two rules, the first was that they should each take a turn at operating the computer and the second was that they should change chairs in a clockwise rotation after each turn. These rules help enormously with both quiet children and gender problems. Hoyles also expresses this concern

(Hoyles, 1988, pp. 1, 5–11). My experiences have also shown that as girls grow in confidence their self-esteem also grows and they become more assertive and will take the lead.

During this activity the children worked as a team and co-operated well together. The following transcript illustrates how they all participated in the discussion:

Chris	That's it, now we've got to go forward, about, how much? 20.
Joanna	40.
Ryan	50.
Lisa	It'll go too far, [pause] but it doesn't matter.
Shvetal	I'll write it for you [uses 50].
Chris	. . . [short pause] Err! If it goes forward then you can go along, can't you!

All the children interacted, often there were half and unfinished sentences, but always the discussion was about solving the problem.

Group 1 began with the children telling me about their favourite toys. Courtney's was a talking doll, Jodie's a pink teddy called Rose, Steven's a radio-controlled car, Matthew's a blue train called Gordon, Stevie's a transformer, Glen's an electric train set, and my favourite toy was big trak (my big trak is extremely battered and is normally replaced by a roamer[2]).

This then led into using big trak. The idea was to drive it into a garage. The children worked hard with plenty of interaction. At the end of the session they were asked what they had liked about my favourite toy (big trak).

Steven	BRILLIANT! [pause] Er, it, um, I liked it because it done, it went so good.
Stevie	It's good.
Jodie	I liked it 'cos it's got buttons on.
Courtney	I liked it because it done a wheel spin.
Steven	Yer, it done a good wheel spin, and I liked it when it went [followed by car noises].
Matthew	I liked when it went round.
Glen	I liked it when it shot, SHOT! [he then demonstrates by typing in the instructions to make big trak shoot].
Steven	There's a light.
Stevie	I didn't see it [he demonstrates so that the rest of the children can see the light] . . .

The girls in Group 2 started work on a similar problem to that started by Group 3 in stage one. They related the activity to their topic of 'air and flight' and called their game 'Circuits and Bumps'. The girls organized themselves quickly and started the process of estimating the distances and angles that were required to complete the activity.

Claire	I'll type it in. Shall we go forward?
Sarah	Yes.
Claire	Forward 1?
Sarah	No, you can't go forward 1 [pause, then suggests] 50.
Claire	No, what do you want? [to Alaina]
Alaina	40, forward 40 [Claire types in forward 40] . . .

They were all involved throughout, but at this stage their estimations were way ou
Forward 250 would have been a more realistic suggestion. As the game progressed the
decided that they were in a mess and started again. By break time they had becom
more accurate with their estimations. They worked through their break and recorde
where they were up to before they returned to their class.

In the meantime the boys had problems with translating the routes that they ha
written down into scale drawings. Not deterred, they worked on and completed th
task with some help.

In contrast Group 3 had organized themselves into groups, got straight down t
work, and applied strategies for completing the tasks that they had set each othe
Although the work was similar, the children were happy with this problem and wer
working at a level appropriate to themselves. They needed to establish some basi
concepts before they could progress on to more advanced work.

The girls worked hard at the computer and made appropriate decisions.

Joanna   50 is an even number.

Not only were they operating at a higher level than the younger children in Group :
but they were using concepts and knowledge that they had acquired on previou
occasions to help them in their decision processes.

The reception children (Group 1) continued to work well with big trak. They were a
this stage able to estimate distances accurately. Together we produced images of
house and a petrol station on large sheets of paper. These acted as a focus for th
session's activities. The children controlled big trak so that it went from the house t
the petrol station and back in turn. The next stage was to use Logo on the computer

During the next stage there were two computers available, thus enabling the tw
groupings within Group 2 to get on with the game ('Circuits and Bumps') simultar
eously. They found it easier. However, the children needed some encouragement t
help them realize that statements could be rationalized:

Dr Griffin   Oh! that looks interesting. What happened?
Richard   We typed forward 300, then back 200, then back 20.
Matthew   'Cos it went round the screen.
Dr Griffin   . . . [pause] . . . What could we have typed instead of forward 30(
                 then back 200, then back 20?

There was some discussion, after which . . .

Adam   FORWARD 80, . . .

This problem then allowed discussion of the concept of the inverse operation (und
ing). The children were quick to point out that forward 100 could be undone by bac
100 and that left 55°could be undone by right 55°.

The reception class (Group 1) started the session with a demonstration of th
Turtle,[2] followed by role play. They took it in turns to be the Turtle while I gave the
instructions.

Dr Griffin   Forward four paces.
Everybody   One . . . Two . . . Three . . . Four.
Dr Griffin   Back two paces.

Everybody	One . . . Two.
Dr Griffin	How far has Stevie gone?

Pause, while they think . . .

Courtney	I think he has gone six paces.
Steven	I think two paces . . .

Who was right? – both answers were certainly valid! In one case (Courtney's) the total distance travelled was given, and in the other (Steven's) the resultant distance that had been travelled in the forward direction had been given. The answer that I had been hoping for was two paces. But both children deserved and got credit for their answers.

After all of the children had had a turn, they were shown how to use the keyboard so that they could control the Turtle. They then took it in turns to make the Turtle go forwards and backwards.

Over the remainder of my time with this group they worked hard and enjoyed working with the Turtle. Their skills (keyboarding and ability to estimate) improved considerably. From time to time we digressed to discuss what we had done, to do some art work and to use big trak. Time was too short to explore the curricular opportunities that presented themselves while we were exploring Logo.

An important aspect of the work was for the children to be able to pass on to their peers what we had done. This was done by each group having a class assembly, and in the case of the reception children two class assemblies. These assemblies were impromptu events, done in the school library, in which the children talked about what they had been doing, demonstrated Logo and the Turtle, and showed their art work. The highlight for me was when Jodie (one of the reception children) demonstrated how to use the Turtle. She typed in the commands (back, forward, etc.) with confidence, enthusiasm and eyes sparkling with excitement. She was keen to move on to the next activity after completing the demonstration. Her enthusiasm was certainly contagious, and made my day.

I found the experience of working towards continuity and a spiral curriculum to be valuable. The major drawback which I experienced was that none of the groups had any experience of Logo. This situation is typical of many primary schools at the current time. It underlines the need to work towards continuity and to have a coherent plan for achieving continuity over a number of years. For the short term, all ages will be doing similar things (as in my piece of research), but increasingly there will be a need to build on what the children have done and to explore other aspects of Logo. In the short term, I feel that I have demonstrated with this piece of research that aspects of Logo can be repeated by children of differing ages and that it is possible to pitch the work at the varying levels in order that educational benefit can be derived by all – indeed, the notion of the spiral curriculum can clearly be applied to this aspect of Logo.

Conclusion

In terms of learning, both the children and I were able to explore 'learning discovery systems' and benefit from the experience. In the second case study, on Logo, we were able to work with microworlds.

Working in Turtle microworlds is a model for what it is to get to know an idea the way that you get to know a person. Students who work in these environments certainly do discover facts, make propositional generalizations, and learn skills. But the primary learning experience is not one of memorizing facts or of practicing skills. Rather it is getting to know the Turtle, exploring what a turtle can and cannot do. It is similar to the child's everyday activities, such as making mud pies and testing the limits of parental authority – all of which have a component of 'getting to know'.
(Papert, 1982, p. 136)

We were all subject to growth. But in particular the growth of the children could measured and demonstrated by their increasing independence, by their ability internalize events, and their being able to communicate to others the learning that h been experienced.

Through these case studies it has been my aim to illustrate how 'control technolog and 'Logo' fit comfortably into the domain of 'Learning Discovery Systems in t Computerized Classroom'.

I enjoyed my attempts at teaching, and I was clearly reminded of the everyd pressures on teachers and of the demands placed on them by children, parents, t school, the Local Education Authority, worsening conditions of service, the Natior Curriculum and other curriculum initiatives, and the list goes on, and on . . .

I was particularly happy with the help and support that I was given by the staff at t school, for without them it would all have been nought. The relationship that I ha with the school continues, and it is rewarding to see that the ripple I caused has ma the occasional wave, and that my work within the school has had some influence their current practice.

NOTES

1. Big trak is a toy vehicle that can be programmed by a keyboard and is particularly useful Key Stage 1. It was produced by MB Electronics, Reevesland Industrial Estate, Newpo Gwent.
2. The roamer is a dome-shaped vehicle that can be programmed by a keyboard with Logo-li commands. It is particularly useful at Key Stage 1. Produced by Valiant Technology Limit Gulf House, 370 Old York Road, Wandsworth, London, SW18 1SP.
3. A Turtle is a device that is connected to a computer for use with the Logo program in order demonstrate the program in a more concrete way. It is particularly useful when working w young children and it is sometimes referred to as the Floor Turtle.

Chapter 7

Issues of Multimedia in the Learning Environment

Jon Griffin

Introduction

It is now just over a decade since the Computers in Primary Schools initiative was announced. During the early 1980s computers were predominantly used for 'drill and practice' type activities and were little more than the teaching machines of the 1960s. Although it is still the case that many computer programs are 'subject specific', there has been a growth in the use of 'content free' programs, such as Logo, word processors and spreadsheets, which enable problem-solving activities to be carried out.

More recently, the National Curriculum has been introduced with a view to raising academic standards within our schools and to give consistency to the curriculum across the country. This curriculum recognizes the importance of information technology (IT). Dearing has recently said that IT should underpin the curriculum. In a sense he is only following the line set by others, including Baker, who stated that

> The whole purpose of the Government's . . . proposals for schools is to raise standards. We must make sure that the curriculum offered to our children is the best that we can devise and entirely appropriate to their needs. We must ensure that full and proper assessment takes place as a check on the performance of both children and their schools. And we must make sure that we use the most modern methods in delivering the curriculum. Information Technology has an important role to play in all these areas. There is every reason to suppose that Information Technology can help to transform education as it has already transformed the commercial and industrial world.
> (Baker, 1989)

With this significant development and the increase in the profile of IT, there are major requirements for initiatives within initial teacher education courses, staff development programmes for practising teachers, and research at all levels of the education service for IT.

The National Curriculum is a major catalyst for much that takes place in education. Among its problems are that it is not stable, and as a consequence places great demands on all within the education service in coping with the constant changes, and, secondly, that it has made for a heavy and overburdened timetable for staff and pupils alike in

trying to fulfil the requirements of teaching and learning, assessment, a
administration.

The National Curriculum requires that

> Pupils should be able to use Information Technology to:
>
> - communicate and handle information;
> - design, develop, explore and evaluate models of real or imaginary situations;
> - measure and control physical variables and movement.
>
> They should be able to make informed judgements about the application and importance
> of Information Technology, and its effect on the quality of life.
> (DES, 1990b, p. 43)

In practice this means that pupils will use word processors, desk-top publishi
packages, graphics facilities, and sound programs for 'communicating informatio
databases and spreadsheets for 'handling information'; adventure programs, sprea
sheets, turtle graphics and Logo, and simulations for 'modelling'; and control techn
logy applications. These applications tend to be 'content free' in nature, thus giving t
teacher and the learner greater control, freedom and, most importantly, a sense
ownership of the use and content of the learning material. They also tend to allow f
the development of problem-solving activities and strategies, as well as encouragi
collaborative learning situations.

As I have argued in the chapter on 'Learning Discovery Systems', the underlyi
thinking for these activities is based on an image of the child as an epistemologist; t
supports Piaget's view that children are active builders of their own intellectu
structures (Papert, 1982). So it is with computers. Children can experiment, find o
and use their experiences and other cues to solve new problems.

Since the advent of the microcomputer in the late 1970s there has been a significa
growth in the amount of computer activity being done at all levels within our schoo
This activity has two foci, one being a subject study for which some 100,000 candida
in schools sit examinations each year, the other being a cross curricula tool in which t
computer is used to support and enhance learning across a range of subjects and acr
the complete age range.

It is therefore not surprising that the use of IT features within 'teacher trainir
courses and that the Council for the Accreditation of Teacher Education raised t
profile of IT by insisting that all courses which prepare students for a career in teachi
must contain an element of IT. Indeed, the requirement is that

> On completion of their course, all students should be able to select and make appropriate
> use of a range of equipment and resources to promote learning. In particular, all courses
> should contain compulsory and clearly identifiable elements which enable students to
> make effective use of Information Technology in the classroom and provide a sound basis
> for their subsequent development in this field. They should be able to:
>
> - make confident personal use of a range of software packages and Information
>   Technology devices appropriate to their subject specialism and age range;
> - review critically the relevance of software packages and Information Technology
>   devices to their subject specialism and age range and judge the potential value of
>   these in classroom use;
> - make constructive use of Information Technology in their teaching and in particular
>   prepare and put into effect schemes of work incorporating appropriate uses of
>   Information Technology;

- evaluate the ways in which the use of Information Technology changes the nature of teaching and learning.

(DES, 1990b, p. 43)

This approach places a great responsibility on training institutions which are already trying to fit a 'quart' into a 'pint pot', but which are taking these demands seriously. For example, we at Anglia Polytechnic University provide modules in IT for *all* students in all years of our degree programmes for primary students. In addition, we provide optional modules in IT which all students are free to choose, as well as offering Technology as a subject specialism which students can elect to do as one of two main subjects.

An Exciting Time for Educational Computing

Among other things, the National Curriculum requires that pupils are able to manipulate text, graphics, sound and video. This brings an exciting new dimension to IT, as the possibilities for developing interactive multimedia systems for use in our classrooms are opened up by the advent of powerful modern computers and their ability to control text, graphics, sound and video with relative ease and at a low cost.

> It is an exciting time for educational computing. We have behind us now more than ten years of experience with this medium. We have accomplished some great successes and accumulated a number of failures. We are no longer as naive as we once were, and yet we are still idealistic enough to keep trying out some wildly new things.
> (Ambron and Hooper, 1990, p. 7)

I wish that I had said these profound words. They sum up how I feel about the industry that I work in, and for my profession as a teacher educator with a special interest in computer education.

Interactive multimedia is one of these 'exciting and wildly new things'. Researchers have been developing systems which are suitable for use in teacher education and primary school classrooms. Leaders in this field include Ambron (Apple Computers, in the USA) and Heppell (Anglia Polytechnic University). Although the extension of their work into primary schools can be clearly seen, the focus of their work, and that of others, has been very much at an academic level and aimed at researchers, educators in higher education, the corporate market, and the production of multimedia products on compact discs.

My interest in this area is the extension of Ambron and Heppell's work into both teacher training and the primary classroom.

I first encountered computers within the education system in 1974, and although I had been involved with them for a long time prior to that, as an engineer, I am still excited by the new possibilities that they offer to the education system – 'interactive multimedia' is one of these new and exciting things!

That first experience of computers within schools was when I worked in a large mixed comprehensive school in Newcastle upon Tyne with a group of upper sixth form A-level mathematics pupils. I taught computer programming to this group. The processing of the programs was predominantly done by coding them on to punched cards and feeding the cards into an IBM 360/370 computer at Newcastle Polytechnic – the whole of this process took a week, and there was no guarantee that the program would work. Errors could be caused by mistakes by the programmer or by typing errors as the cards were

prepared by the punch-card operators. Thus it was not uncommon for even the simpl
of computer programs to take several weeks before they would work properly a
produce the necessary output for the students.

In addition to this facility for 'batching' programs at Newcastle Polytechnic, t
school had a remote terminal which it shared with three other secondary schools. T
meant that the teletype terminal was only in the school for five days each month. Th
when schools complain about inadequate resourcing today, it is clear that by t
standards of the 1970s they are extremely well-resourced. Of course, since t
development of the microcomputer in the late 1970s there has been a major brea
through in educational computing, and with the associated resourcing; however
would not like to suggest that schools are adequately resourced – far from it! Althou
we are moving towards the position of every classroom having its own computer, the
is every evidence to suggest that schools are inadequately resourced in hardwa
software and human terms for delivering the curriculum of the 1990s, and, as H
(1990) argues, there is still a long way to go before this area of work is fully recogniz
and properly resourced.

At about the same time I wrote a program for 'addition and subtraction' which I us
with junior school children. By today's standards this was a simple and clun
program, but it was a first step in primary computing, and along with many ot
innovations it has led to the position in IT that we see in schools today.

In the 1970s the focus of computing in schools was on computer programming a
computer studies. In the ten-year period from 1974 to 1983 the number of pup
entered by schools for public examinations at all levels from the Certificate
Secondary Education to the General Certificate of Education at Advanced Level r
from just under 7,000 to in excess of 100,000 (DES, 1990a). This level of entries is s
being maintained today, although under other guises such as IT. Indeed, the level
activity was remarkable in view of the fact that the first electronic computer had o
been invented in the mid-1940s and the first commercial computer had been installed
1953 (for Lyon's Tea Houses).

The National Curriculum

In addition to this high level of computing activity as an examination subject with
secondary schools there has been a significant development of computing across t
curriculum, both in the secondary and primary phases of education. Most of this h
taken place in the period from 1983 to the present time. Indeed, with the advent of t
National Curriculum there is now a clearly definable element of computing that m
be taught within schools.

By the end of the 1980s the term 'computing' had been replaced by 'informati
technology' – this is the term used within the National Curriculum!

> Information Technology has a critical role in enhancing the learning process at all levels
> and across a broad range of activities including but going beyond the National Curriculum.
> Through the use of Information Technology in the curriculum, schools will also be helping
> pupils become knowledgeable about the nature of information, comfortable with the new
> technology and able to exploit its potential.
> (DES, 1989a, para. 7)

With the advent of the National Curriculum we saw a great momentum in the use of IT on two fronts.

First, at the time of the inception of the National Curriculum the Secretary of State for Education insisted that all subject working parties should incorporate IT within their subject areas (Baker, 1989). Thus, for example, those parts of IT appropriate to mathematics would be found within the mathematics curriculum and those parts of IT appropriate to English would be found within the English curriculum.

Second, IT would be a subject in its own right. An investigation of the Technology National Curriculum document reveals that this subject area contains two subjects, namely 'Design and Technology Capability' and 'Information Technology Capability'. Although contained within one document, these two components are seen as separate subjects which are cross-curricular in nature and should be taught as an integral part of most foundation subjects in primary and secondary schools. In reality, they should be contained in separate documents. 'The reference to "capability" in both components emphasizes that technology is a subject concerned with practical action, drawing on knowledge and understanding from a wide range of subjects. (DES, 1990b).

Information Technology Capability within the National Curriculum is about:

- communicating and handling information;
- designing, developing, exploring and evaluating models of real or imaginary situations;
- measuring physical quantities and controlling movement;
  making informed judgements.

As stated earlier, it means that word processors, databases, spreadsheets, graphics and desk-top publishing packages will play an important role along with activities such as programming in Logo and control technology within the technology curriculum.

In essence, the National Curriculum also requires that all pupils should be able to handle and manipulate *text*, *images* and *sound*. When these activities are combined with the activities of communicating and handling information we have the ingredients for 'interactive multimedia' in the learning environment.

With the advent of low-cost computers, the scope for powerful learning packages which put the learner in a position to be able to control and direct the learning environment has opened up new horizons and requires imagination and new skills by those who are designing learning packages, those who are using them in their teaching, and the learners. Such low-cost computers put us in the position to be able to deliver the curriculum as defined by the National Curriculum in a variety of exciting ways. One of these is through the use of multimedia techniques.

New Learning Environments

As Ambron says, trying to define multimedia is like 'Defining the Undefinable' (Barker and Tucker 1990, p. 18). However, many statements can be made about the subject, and experiences had of multimedia environments, which slowly give one an understanding of multimedia and the capabilities of differing multimedia systems.

Multimedia techniques can be used to create a wide variety of interactive learni environments. These environments can be designed in such a way that learni processes are learner-controlled, interactive, and highly motivating. In the 1960s a '70s multimedia meant a learning package which included an audio cassette, or vide and text. Today it has come to mean much more. We are coming to the conclusion th in the 1990s computers and their ability for advanced information-processing tec niques are central to multimedia and that the term interactive is closely associated with

As in desk-top publishing packages one can combine text and graphics, so multimedia packages one can combine text, speech, music, sounds of all kinds, imag and video. ' "Interactive Multimedia" is a collection of computer-centred technologi that give a user the capability to access and manipulate text, sounds, and image (Ambron and Hooper, 1990, p. xi).

Although there has been a range of media for use in education for many decades, it only recently, with the advent of powerful modern computers and appropriate autho ing systems, that multimedia techniques in the learning environment have started develop. The next part of this chapter attempts to give a definition of multimedia, investigate Hypercard as an authoring system, to look at the issues that multimedia h for the learning environment, and to draw some conclusions regarding the impact multimedia on the learning environment.

Multimedia techniques can be used to create a variety of learning environmen environments which are usually designed in such a way that the learning processes a controlled by the learner, are interactive and participative, and are highly motivatin

Central to the multimedia environment is some sort of computer. The computer interfaced to a range of devices which are used to effect the presentation of the learni material (e.g., text, graphics, animations and sound), collect student responses a behavioural data, and make the learning experience more active, participative a motivating.

Text is a fundamental part of any system, and is used extensively within mc learning materials and is commonly compiled with the aid of word-processing pac ages. It is and will continue to be one of the primary mechanisms for preserving a presenting learning material. However, when using text one needs to take into accou a whole range of issues, issues which affect its production, readability, meaning, a the imagery that is to be conveyed by the written word. Consider the effects on t written word caused by the use of screen (or page) layout and design. The use of whi space, differing fonts in a range of sizes and styles, graphics and video, and the use sounds, all contribute to the imagery portrayed by text.

For instance, note how the following verse (Haywood, 1969), when typed in the 'S. Francisco' font (fig. 7.1), conveys a light-hearted feeling, but in contrast, wh presented in the 'Times' font (fig. 7.2), conveys a serious feeling.

One should also consider the advantages (and disadvantages) of using a screen display text rather than using paper.

> On paper the text is just there, in the same way and at the same place, whenever you look at it. On a screen text may appear and disappear. It may stand still or move. It may present itself page-wise or roll-wise. Depending upon the speed of presentation it may creep slowly over the page, or it may appear so quickly that you notice almost nothing more than a change from blankness to a full-sized page of letters.
> (Waern and Rollenhagen in Barker, 1989, p. 23)

I never thought I'd live to be a hundred
I never thought I'd get to do the things
That all those other souls do, and they do.

I never thought I'd live to be a hundred
I never thought I'd get to do the things
That all those other souls do, and they do.

Figure 7.1 *The effect on imagery by altering the font. The use of 'San Francisco' conveys a light-hearted feeling.*

Figure 7.2 *The effect on imagery by altering the font. The use of 'Times' conveys a serious feeling.*

These comments illustrate the potential advantages of screen text over its paper equivalent. Other advantages include the spontaneity in updating ideas or information, the ability to react to inputs from the learner, and the opportunities it offers for incorporating special effects.

By being able to update ideas and information, the meaning of the text can be made relevant to other things that are taking place. By reacting to inputs from the user the computer is able to enable other things to happen, such as providing further information, carrying out spell checks, or jumping to another area of text. Special effects can be built in which enhance the meaning or imagery portrayed by the text – one example of this use of special effects would be to have the San Francisco font in figure 7.1 fade slowly into the Times font used in figure 7.2.

The use of computer graphics is a significant feature, and one often wonders if this is a help or a hindrance. There are occasions when seeing a picture of some object or scene can be a distinct disadvantage. It may be that the author intends the reader to create their own imagery. In cases such as this the absence of pictures is appropriate. There is, however,

> a significant volume of evidence to support the use of imagery as an educationally useful medium within a variety of different training and learning situations. Indeed, it is now quite well established that images and pictorial data play an important role in:
>
> - determining the way in which individuals perceive their external environment;
> - facilitating mechanisms of memory and recall;
> - influencing the efficiency with which people are able to communicate with each other and with computers.
>
> (Barker, 1989, p. 26)

Barker goes on to cite Barker and Najah (1985), Barker and Skipper (1986), Barnett (1981), Neurath (1939 and 1980), and Paivio (1980) as sources of evidence for these claims. These claims are further supported by the research and development activities currently taking place, together with the large amounts of computer software for instructional and learning purposes which effectively use graphics within them to aid the assimilation of information.

The term 'computer graphics' encompasses any technique that enables a computer system to generate pictures. At its simplest it involves graphics programs which enable images to be produced on the screen by drawing techniques involving the keyboard and mouse. These images can be used directly, modified, or enhanced by graphics packages. Most computer systems have files of images which can be used to illustrate courseware. Figure 7.3 shows how images produced in this way can add to the imagery of the written word. An extension is the use of digitizers which can scan images into the computer's memory. In addition to being able to display static images on the screen, it is a relatively easy process to animate images and thus add to the meaning portrayed in this way.

Titchy Witch

My friends would call me titchy witch
I said, "I wasn't small"
But when they called me witchy titch
I didn't speak at all
I just raised my hands and thought a spell
And they're tiny now, as well

Figure 7.3 *The effect on imagery by adding icons and pictures to text (poem by Samuel Hiscock, graphics by Valli Twinley).*

The technology is now with us to enable devices capable of showing film strips, slides and video to be interfaced and controlled by a computer system. Of these, the video and the compact disc player are perhaps the most significant. Video technology offers a powerful tool for capturing 'reality' for subsequent use in learning packages. Having these video images on a disc rather than on tape means there is a significant increase in access speeds and in the effect of the video material on the learning environment, thus making video disc a far more useful medium than video tape. A typical video system can provide almost instant access to any of 30,000 images, images which can be shown as static or video sequences. By the use of special effects it is possible to combine images from a video disc with material that has been generated by the computer system such as text, graphics and sound.

Audio techniques encompass a wide range of resources such as voice synthesizers, music synthesizers, voice recognition equipment, and compact disc players. With the advances in sound-processing techniques, voice synthesis now has a realistic quality and need no longer have the 'robotics' effect that we are all familiar with. Indeed, with the use of low-cost recorders it is possible to record, edit and play back any sounds including the human voice, music, and special effects.

Teaching . . . and learning have traditionally been people oriented activities. Therefore any discussion of the pedagogical applications of computers should take into account the

basic nature of human communication. Humans are naturally multi-channel communic-ators. That is they use a number of communication channels (often simultaneously) to get across and receive messages.
(Barker, 1989, p. 32)

Earlier in this chapter I looked at the components, or channels (text, images, and sound), that in conjunction with a computer make up a multimedia system. If we were to consider the example of a conversation between two people, we might note the following activities or processes taking place. During the conversation communication takes place by speech, writing, sketching and drawing of one form or another, touch, eye movement, facial expression, gesticulation, and other body language. Each of these activities relates to a channel and conveys specific information or adds clarifica-tion or meaning to the information being conveyed. Often more than one channel will be used simultaneously.

When a computer is used as a medium for teaching and learning, much of the information conveyed by the various channels available to humans is lost. However, with the advent of powerful modern computers we have the opportunity to emulate many of these features, and by integrating text, images and sound with a computer we are able to create an interactive multimedia system which can provide multiple communication channels. Due to the complexity of such systems, there is a need for authoring systems that allow learning packages to be developed with the minimum of fuss and effort.

Multimedia Systems

For many the technicalities of developing material of one kind or another will be irrelevant, as their sole concern is the use of good quality multimedia software, which is becoming more and more readily available and often comes on compact discs, thus requiring computers which have available compact disc players and speaker systems. Others will be interested in developing their own learning material for use with children or, more importantly, will want children to develop material using multimedia techniques.

Within a typical multimedia system there are two parts. One part is used for developing materials such as learning packages and the other is used for presenting them. In some cases a component may be used both for the development and the presentation of a learning package.

The minimum requirements in order to develop material are a computer (with, typically, a minimum of 4MB of internal memory and a hard disk) and an authoring package such as HyperCard. Optionally, other programs can be used (such as a word processor for producing and editing text, and graphics programs for producing and editing images prior to inserting them into the material under development). There are also a range of devices that can be used to capture images and sound. These devices include scanners and the associated software for digitizing photographs, drawings and illustrations, which can then be used directly or modified by graphics programs before being used; a recorder or microphone and associated software for entering sound into the system; an interactive video player complete with interactive video discs and associated software; a compact disc player complete with compact discs and associate software.

Developing Learning Materials

In order to present packages, whether they are developed by the user or by a publishin company, a typical multimedia system might include a computer with a minimum 4MB of internal memory and a hard disk, the appropriate software, a compact dis player and appropriate compact discs, an interactive video player and interactive vide discs, and possibly display systems that will allow the material to be used with larg audiences.

The excitement and joy of using multimedia is to be able develop multi-chann systems which go beyond sequential systems into the domain of parallel processing an thus are nearer to the multi-channelled interactive system of two humans carrying out conversation that was described earlier.

Having defined multimedia and looked at a number of channels that make it up, it worth considering some of the issues involved in creating multimedia learning materia

Within the Apple Macintosh environment a commonly used authoring system fc developing multimedia environments is HyperCard. As Semper says, HyperCard is software package which 'serves as a framework for learning. The HyperCard structu actually mimics some of our thinking processes. For one thing, it tends to involv manipulating bite-sized pieces of information – a graphic, a sound, an image' (Ambrc and Hooper, 1990, p. 56).

HyperCard can be considered as a set of cards which can contain text, graphics an sound, and which can control external devices such as a compact disc player, or combination of these and other effects. These cards can be sequenced so that they g from one to another in such a way that the user is unaware that they are indeed separat cards. A whole range of special effects is available, making HyperCard an ideal tool fc developing learning material.

As Hooper observes, these and other 'equally compelling pedagogical properties (HyperCard made it, from its inception, an exciting tool for use in creating learnir presentations and in creating tools that could be used for learning' (Ambron an Hooper, 1990, p. 15). Indeed, like Hooper, I now feel inadequate if I have to make presentation to a large group without supporting it with a multimedia presentation.

In many texts HyperCard and multimedia are treated as interchangeable. I go alor with this in so far as HyperCard is a software tool which enables multiple channels to t programmed easily. However, in many applications HyperCard is seen as the begir ning and the end, and thus it falls short of a multimedia environment. Mintz sugges four ways for using HyperCard (multimedia) in education:

> By the teacher for the teacher: Record keeping, generating forms, keeping personal business, having fun, learning what it is like to learn something new.
> By the teacher for the children: Setting up computer-learning stations [I prefer the term setting up computer-learning situations], preparing demonstrations, creating record keeping stacks for children to use, cataloging whole curriculums, teaching programming and database management, controlling laser disc and compact disc players.
> By the children for the children: Learning to program, having fun, making tools for themselves.

By the children for the teacher and the classroom: Storytelling, creating animation, managing a database, doing presentations, gathering and sorting information for reports, developing art projects, controlling external devices such as laser disc and compact disc players.
(Ambron and Hooper, 1990, pp. 157–8)

I think Mintz's later comments about HyperCard are profound and fit well with my own view when he says, 'HyperCard is an incredible tool in the hands of users who are willing to understand and use it . . . it is not easy . . . it is not always logical and fun . . . it is not a complete educational package . . . Still, it is a step in the right direction' (Ambron and Hooper, 1990, pp. 158–9). This hints at future developments, but brings us 'down to earth' and reminds us that a lot of time, effort and hard work need to be employed when developing learning materials.

When creating learning material it is important to focus on the learning activities and experiences rather than on the processes involved in creating the learning materials. It is easy to focus on multimedia techniques rather than on the learners.

This tendency to concentrate on a computer, physically in front of you, and to become immersed in the intricacies of software development is a natural one, because the learners are physically remote, are personally unknown and their learning processes unknown.
(Riley, 1990, p. 17)

There are many ways of learning about a given topic, and similar information could be presented as reference material, drill and practice exercises to be completed and assessed, self-study tutorials, and simulations.

Indeed, within these materials a variety of techniques for questioning can be used such as directed, closed, or open-ended questions. Although learning materials based on the above styles could cover similar material, it is quite clear that the style and make-up would be very different in each case. Thus it is important to consider what the learners will do and how they will achieve these objectives before commencing on the development of any learning material. Indeed, whether a computer is required needs to be questioned!

When researching specific lessons and learning experiences, ask teachers questions such as:

- Are learners expected to memorise factual information, rehearse skills, perform tasks, identify problems, make decisions, communicate results?
- How should learners use their computers to help with their tasks and activities?
- Will learners work on their own, in small groups, or will they watch teacher-led demonstrations?

(Riley, 1990, p. 17)

As the learning material is developed, one has to consider teaching ideologies and styles. Typical ideologies and styles might include teacher-centred learning based on class presentations, individualized learning based on drill and practice activities, group work in which learners are encouraged to collaborate with each other, problem-solving and guided discovery techniques, the use of open-ended questions or, more likely, a combination of these and other styles. Riley (1990, pp. 19–22) goes on to outline a range of commonly used strategies for learning in a way that enables software designers to grasp these issues and put them into context.

One guiding principle for developing multimedia learning material is that it is easy to use and helps learners feel satisfied and rewarded for their efforts. If learners find the material confusing, unpredictable or frustrating, it is likely that it needs redesigning There are clearly a number of principles that form the basis for the production of 'good learning material. I should stress that each learning material is individual and unique and therefore the way that the principles are interpreted will vary to take into account the special nature of individual pieces of learning material.

The following principles are suggested by Riley:

- *Know the users.*
- Encourage active learning.
- Make stacks [learning materials] easy to understand.
- Make stacks [learning materials] easy to use.
- Give control to learners.
- Reassure learners.
- Test, test, and test again. (Riley, 1990, p. 29)

Although in some cases it is fairly obvious what Riley means by these principles, it i worth reviewing them briefly to clarify their meaning.

In 'knowing the users' it is important to be aware of the learners' ability, age an interests. In addition to knowing the learner, the material and the context in which th material is to be used, it is important to be familiar with the style of learning that is to b employed.

In encouraging 'active learning' it is important to devise activities which will involv and challenge the learner. These activities should then be built into the learnin material in such a way that they will support and encourage learning – it is crucial t decide what the learners will do before you decide what the learning material will do

All too often computer-based learning material is unintelligible, difficult to use an irrelevant, thus discouraging the learner from using it or any other computer-base material. Riley regularly uses the term 'stack' – a term which readily translates t 'learning material' or 'a piece of learning material' depending on the context in which i is used. Making learning material 'easy to understand' and 'easy to use' is important To do this it is essential to 'help learners form a mental model of what a stack does an how it may contribute to their [learners'] intentions and goals. The stack, through it own appearance and behaviour, should indicate to the learners how it may be used (Riley, 1990, p. 26).

We enjoy feeling 'in control' of our own destinies, and so it is with learning materia The learner should feel in control and should be taking the initiative, formulating plan and actions, and making decisions and choices rather than responding to the dictates o the computer. Part of this feeling of being in control is that the 'learners need to b reassured'.

> Educational stacks should seem safe and reliable to learners so they need not worry about losing data, wasting their time or getting lost . . .
> Learners should feel in control of the computer and confident their work is in 'safe hands'. A stack should be physically stable in the sense of being crash proof or idiot proof and not lose learners' work or corrupt their data. Events like these are immensely frustrating to learners and teachers.
> (Riley, 1990, p. 32)

The principle of 'test, test, and test again' is so important. There is nothing worse tha a computer program or computer-based learning material that has 'bugs' or errors i it. Many good ideas have been degraded by design omissions, programming errors and typographical errors that could have easily been found if the material had been properly tested. Part of this testing process is to have the material reviewed by people who have not been involved in its development, to look for features which detract from the material, and to look for features which will enhance and improve the quality of the learning that takes place when using the material.

Ambron and Hooper (1990), Barker and Tucker (1990), Barker (1989), and Riley (1990) give some useful guidelines for the design of multimedia learning material. These guidelines clearly reflect and support the principles of design for multimedia learning materials covered in this chapter, such as the planning and organization of the design process, the organization of learning material, the use of visual effects, programming techniques and strategies, the layout and structure of learning material, the use of graphics and illustrations, and the use of text and data. It is not my intention to go over all of these issues again. However, I feel it would be useful to emphasize two points which have helped me in designing learning material:

First of all, many of us go through a series of meetings and brainstorming sessions during the planning and organization of a project and then omit to set aside time for researching and reviewing the work of others in order that this work can inform our own efforts – how often have we reinvented the wheel as a consequence of this lack of research? It is essential that this time is invested!

Second, we need to remind ourselves that learners have a great deal of prior knowledge and experience to bring to any new learning experience, as Riley says in relation to stacks (learning material):

> learners come to a stack with many years of accumulated knowledge and experience. Build on this to make a stack easy to use. . . . [A] well chosen metaphor or form of presentation helps learners form a coherent, mental picture of what the stack is, what it does and what it does not do.
> (Riley, 1990, p. 44)

Multimedia: The Future

The final section in this chapter on the 'Issues of Multimedia in the Learning Environment' comments on some of the exciting developments that are taking place.

I am privileged to have Stephen Heppell as a colleague. Stephen is the UK's leading expert on multimedia systems and leads a team of researchers at Anglia Polytechnic University specifically to look at the 'New Learning Environment' within education. He is involved in many national and international projects, which include:

- Setting up an 'UltraLab' (a unit which contains experts in education and multimedia, all the latest technology, work areas, and classrooms) for researchers and educators to use in developing skills in the use of multimedia techniques.
- Setting up and co-ordinating a project on, 'A Day in the Life of . . . ', which will follow young people in countries across Europe for a day and will result in a multimedia learning package.
- Creating a range of learning packages. The first significant one was 'Broken Calculator' (Heppell, 1991) – a program which displays an electronic calculator on the screen. The calculator operates just like a conventional calculator, with the

exception that the learner is able to 'break' keys, thus being able to set up 'good' problem-solving situations. For example, how do you add 3 to 9 if the '3' key and the '+' key are inoperative? This program then proved the stimulus for developing a whole suite of software for use by primary aged children (5 to 11). This learning material operates through what Stephen calls 'work rooms' and allows the learner access to Broken Calculator, Broken Text, Doodle, a database, and a word processor.

I have also found *The Encyclopaedia of Multimedia*, which was produced by the Multimedia Laboratory (1990). This set of material contains a number of interactive video discs that I have used as sources of images and video sequences within my own developments. The discs range from an Encyclopaedia of Multimedia, through to areas such as the environment, NBC news items on the Holy Land, and Beethoven's Ninth Symphony.

Another useful source of material is the BBC's Doomsday discs (BBC, 1986). These discs were produced to commemorate the original Doomsday Book, which was compiled in 1086, and they contain a compendium of life in Britain in the 1980s, in the form of text, data, statistics, photographs, video material, news items, and a full set of Ordinance Survey maps for Britain. Although the British Broadcasting Corporation co-ordinated this project, schoolchildren throughout Britain were used to collect the information about their local areas.

In this chapter I have provided a context for multimedia in the learning environment; provided a definition of a multimedia system; looked at issues, principles and guide-lines for designing and creating multimedia learning materials; and looked at some developments of multimedia learning material.

It seems clear to me that the advances in computer design and software development have provided opportunities to educators and learners for exploring and realizing the potential that these developments offer to teaching and learning. Jenkins is right when she says:

> technology is shrinking the world into a global society, into a new society built on a knowledge-based economy. The advent of this new era will demand new educational requirements – for development of higher-order thinking skills to effectively utilise the technological tools of the twenty-first century. In effect, we will have to educate a population to think creatively, productively, and prolifically. To adequately prepare a generation for this technology-based information age, we must foster a positive predisposition toward learning. The best entry point for beginning this technological education is with the young child. . . . [O]ne way of doing this is through effective applications of technology.
> (Ambron and Hooper, 1990, p. 113)

Jenkins' view is clearly based on the thinking of Bruner, who states:

> a new breed of development theory is likely to arise . . . its central technical concern will be how to create in the young an appreciation of the fact that many worlds are possible, that meaning and reality are created and not discovered, that negotiation is the art of constructing new meanings by which individuals can regulate their relations with each other.
> (Ambron and Hooper, 1990, p. 113)

It seems to me that HyperCard and the ability to program it for multimodal interactions[1] is at the heart of Bruner's comment, for such systems allow the learner to be able to create and collaborate in a learning environment. Both Bruner and Jenkins highlight the need for beginning with the young child.

The young have no fears of technology, they have been brought up in a technological environment. It is only we adults who fear this technology. Yet it is us adults who have the exciting and often frightening task of using this advanced technology within our teaching.

As a consequence of my enthusiasm for multimedia learning materials and my belief in starting with young children, I have embarked on a research project to develop, evaluate and review a curriculum for teaching students who are training to be primary teachers (i.e., who will deal with 5- to 11-year-olds) about the issues and applications of multimedia in the learning environment – this project is sponsored by industry.

I think Ambron's remarks more than adequately make my final point when she says:

> Education and training is about presenting information and transforming it into knowledge. It is therefore not surprising if many educators and trainers have leaped to the conclusion that interactive multimedia was invented solely for them. Not so! If it were then it probably would not be the revolutionary step that we claim. . . . Interactive multimedia is destined to be the future interface of the next generation.
> (Barker and Tucker, 1990, p. 21)

NOTES

1. Multimodal is used to denote a system with many facets which in this case include the use of text, sound, still images, and video.

Chapter 8

Text, Images and Sound Equals Multimedia

Kara Hales and Steven Russell

Scene One: A primary school staffroom somewhere in Britain. A wet Wednesday lunchtime.

School Information Technology Co-ordinator: Do you want the good news or the even better news?
Technophobic Colleague: [apprehensively] . . . I never trust you when you have that glint in your eye . . . [unwillingly] . . . OK, I'll take the good news.
IT Co-ordinator: Computer technology – through an exciting mix of moving images, sound and text you can manipulate – is going to change the face of your classroom over the next few years.
Colleague: You call that good news? What's wrong with visual aids like the Cuisenaire rods I've been using to teach maths since 1969? . . . [nervously] . . . So what's the even better news?
IT Co-ordinator: Even you'll be able to cope with it.

We've all sat through those TV programmes designed to scare you with 'facts' about what the world will be like in ten or twenty years' time. You know the kind from the late 1970s: a presenter with slicked-back hair and trendy jacket, standing in a chrome-and smoked-glass studio, breathlessly describing how we will soon be driving cars not with a steering wheel but with our brain waves. At home, we'll be sitting back while a robotic manservant caters to our every whim. And, what did we end up with? The Sinclair C5 and Super Mario.

It's easy to scoff. Seriously, the pace of technological change in our lives has been swift. Fortunately, it's been a pace with which we generally appear to have coped mentally. Many of us left school without having seen a computer, let alone being given the opportunity to pound its keyboard and swear when the system goes down. But over just a few short years we've adapted to change and mastered an impressive range of IT skills. If we'd been magically transported from 1968 to 1994, we would have been overwhelmed by the differences we saw, but, because they've happened at a relatively manageable rate, we've taken them in our stride. Multimedia in primary schools, is strikes us, is the proverbial different kettle of fish. Here, the speed of development is so quick that teachers – with more than enough challenges already competing for their attention – are justifiably baffled and consequently resistant to change, either overtly or through apathy and good old human fatigue.

That being said, the worst thing anyone involved in education can do is bury his or her head in the sand when it comes to computerized technology. CD-ROMs are unlikely to be one of those Sinclair C5-style one-day wonders. The momentum appears unstoppable, encouraged by hefty shoves from – unlikely bedfellows though they might seem – both Whitehall decision-makers and supermarket bosses. The National Council for Educational Technology, funded by the Department for Education, has recently placed CD-ROMs and discs in about 10 per cent of the nation's primary schools. Its next step is to marry CD-ROM technology to the National Curriculum, with NCET having commissioned work on thirteen titles devoted to current work in schools. There are estimated to be between 50 and 100 British-produced CD educational titles, with the number expected to grow by 500 per cent by the end of 1994. Down the road at the local foodstore, Tesco has again teamed up with Acorn Computers to run its popular 'Computers for Schools' scheme, in which schools throughout the UK can claim free equipment in exchange for vouchers collected from Tesco shops. This year, revealingly, the scheme has been extended to include CD-ROM.

Exhibit B should convince any doubters among the jury. Frank Glyn-Jones, writing in *The Head's Legal Guide*, states:

> Many teachers report that, where a multimedia PC [Personal computer] is installed, pupils queue up during lunch breaks, stay late or come in early to use it. When it comes to learning, being able to work over points many times, having access to a great amount of information, including original sources, studying animations and flow diagrams, listening to commentaries – all at the individual's finger-tips and at his or her own pace – confirm that multimedia is a tool of extraordinary power.
> (Glyn-Jones, 1994)

He also points out:

> There is much literature about the effect on life-learning patterns that starting structured learning at this [pre-school] age will have. To acquire in the earliest years a familiarity with the technology, and the feeling that learning is fun, will inevitably change the habits of future generations. For example, Mickey's ABCs allows a child to interact on screen while learning the alphabet. When the letter V is pressed, Mickey says 'V is for violin', and he gets up and plays the violin. When the child presses 'O for oven', Mickey opens the oven door and is thrown back by the hot blast. For older children . . . SimCity enables children to create their own city, with fire stations, airports, residential areas and parks. They carefully weigh the health costs of pollution against the expense of nuclear power and railways. Through trial and error, they learn to balance the social, economic and political issues.
> (Glyn-Jones, 1994)

The summing-up in the case of Anxious Teachers vs CD-ROMs is left to Nick Evans, writing in the *Education Guardian*: '[The] CD-ROM is unlikely to replace books as a medium for providing information, but it may well complement them' (Evans, 1994). He argues, that 'an interactive CD can hold on one disc all the volumes normally found in paper form. It can be searched for all references to any topic, it is compact and easy to use – and it's here to stay' (Evans, 1994).

The crucial difficulty for already harassed and wary teachers is that information technology has become a subculture – a society difficult to enter if you don't have the time, energy or inclination to crack its code of jargon and sort out the important details from the peripheral trivia which can baffle an outsider. Take the term CD-ROM, for example. Many long-serving primary school teachers have only a vague idea what it means. Alternatively, however, they probably would understand the concept of a circular chunk of plastic which has words and pictures stored on it that a computer can read and then flash up on its screen. Adverts by computer suppliers generally do little to educate and help the uninitiated. A magazine cover in front of us now bears a flash urging 'SyQuest blowout! Get unlimited hard disk storage with Power User Removable SyQuest drives!' That's fine if you already know what that means, but surely intimi-dates anyone thinking of buying a computer to manage their household accounts.

Some people might think we're on dodgy philosophical ground here, but isn't it time, also, that companies did something about the christening of their products, as a prescription for helping cure the technophobes? Why the obsession with numbers? The man in the street, or the teacher in the classroom, doesn't know an RM 186 from a 486 or an LC 475 Performa Plus from a Quadra 660AV. Don't laugh, but what's wrong with calling a new computer 'The Rainbow', and its updated model 'The Sunrise'? It sounds much friendlier to us than PowerBook 180c 4/160. And that's another thing: much of the language associated with the industry is 'male'. A cursory flick through a magazine throws up 'power pac . . . mega . . . ScanJet . . . impact . . . maximum performance control . . . pro series'. Apart from being jargon, they aren't words aimed at appealing to many women, who represent both a large percentage of existing terminal users and untapped customers. In a similar vein, why are the vast majority of computers white, grey or cream? Many of us would like them in more attractive, easier-on-the-eye pastel shades. Can't computer firms learn from the experiences of Henry Ford?

The media, too, has a lot to answer for, tending to glamorize the industry, rather than attempting to demystify and help IT novices. Running on BBC television at the time of writing is a programme called *The Net*, which appears to be targeted at those with a relatively high degree of knowledge about and interest in computers. A person tuning in with a limited understanding is likely to switch quickly, and gratefully, to *Coronation Street*, or something similar, after being bamboozled by *The Net's* produc-tion style – lots of fast-moving graphics and shots using hand-held cameras that judder about rather than 'holding' their view of a subject.

Even local councils sometimes help perpetuate an unhelpful image of the computer industry, though usually for understandable reasons such as job creation and attempt-ing to bring prosperity to their district: a piece of land next to the dual carriageway that for twenty years has been known locally as an unofficial rubbish dump can suddenly be reborn as a 'technology and science park'. The buildings that spring up are likely to appear futuristic – no inviting mock Tudor constructions here, but windowless, metal-grey edifices, with the company's name mounted on the side in electric blue and neon pink plastic, and a piece of chrome modern-art sculpture out front.

Taken as a whole, the subliminal message received by those not in the know is 'We're smart and work at the cutting edge. We don't mind you joining us, but you've got to know the secret codes and passwords before you can enter our world.'

Surely, however, 'greater familiarity with hardware and software = more users = more profit for the companies'?

As would-be teachers on a Bachelor of Education degree course, we have been swept along by the pace of change. Some of us arrived having never used a computer; others had used them while doing other jobs, but didn't know the ins and outs. Less than fifteen months later, we were all confident and able users of Apple Macs, and other hardware, and could design our own interactive packages. We were luckier than most of the teachers we met during our teaching practices in primary schools: we could develop computing knowledge at our own speed, with helpful lecturers on hand if things went wrong. We also didn't have the day-to-day worry of preparing lessons for thirty children, or controlling a class.

And that's the nub of the multimedia-computing problem as far as most non-technology specializing primary school teachers are concerned: they don't have the freedom to learn through experimentation, as we have, and discover they can use computers to great effect after all.

A friend is in his first teaching job, with a class of 8- and 9-year-olds. His school is one of the 2,297 to be given a computer, CD-ROM drive and samples of CDs by the Government this year as part of a drive to widen multimedia use in education. However, he said:

> It's spent a month sitting on a trolley. No one has yet had the time to work out what it can do, review the software and tell the staff how good it is, or otherwise. Generally, I would say that a third of our teachers, more often than not the older ones, are very intimidated and a bit frightened by computers, and really need some help in overcoming that fear before they can turn to teaching anything substantial. Others who are more broad-minded are not scared by computers, but just can't find the time to spend a day sitting in front of a screen to find out what they could use for a class.

Another acquaintance, who heads the science and technology department at an East Anglian middle school, emphasized his distinction between IT education – developing on-screen skills such as using a mouse, and being able to create databases and spreadsheets – and the use of CDs to locate and manipulate information – with the CD designed to be user-friendly and lead the user down a well-defined, logical path. That's the ideal for makers of educational CDs to meet if they are to extend their influence throughout schools.

For example, one history-based CD, which costs about £70, was aimed at the 9 to 11 age group, but demonstrated many of the potential hazards lurking to trap the unwary in the minefield that is multimedia. Containing a massive 3,000-plus still images and a spoken commentary, it claimed to bring history to life by using colour, movement and sound in a way a book could not. Certainly the CD scores in that it contains a great deal of information that would fill a huge pile of books, and offers a relatively quick on-screen search facility, but both adult and child users found it difficult to investigate the mass of data and would have preferred a more structured approach to have been built in. The text accompanying each picture was generally superficial, and the collection of images would have benefited from savage editing, as many were too similar. Another poor feature was the 'atlas'; clicking the cursor on a place-name brought up a map, with the location marked by a red dot. Unfortunately, the atlas consisted of just one small-scale map, covering Eastern and Western Europe, Scandinavia, and Greenland and Iceland. Clicking on the name of a village in northern England brought a red dot which stretched almost from Hull to Manchester!

We were grateful to the CD designers, who gave us a lot of background information which explained why the product turned out as it did. It began life as a two-country project to produce a laser disc guide to a museum's collection of artefacts. As data was gathered, team members wondered whether they should also produce something more interactive and overtly educational. The problem was that, by then, researchers in different countries were ploughing ahead with their work virtually unshackled. When the material arrived at the CD programmers' offices, they were faced with two five-foot piles – one of text and another of photographic slides – which they had to shoehorn on to a compact disc. One admitted to us that they'd really needed a dictator to give direction to the information-gathering process, rather than trying to edit through a committee structure. By that stage, thoughts of being able to create a truly interactive CD for schools had to be abandoned as unworkable.

Crucially, a prototype had never been put before children for them to 'road test' which would have thrown up most of the difficulties that needed to be sorted out before it went on to the market. Pupils who reviewed the CD for us found it had captured the boring, dusty aspects of history but left behind the excitement of real-life events and figures. They complained there was little flow or cohesion to the material and wanted logical narration to pull together stray strands of information. Those with greater experiences of computer programs and games suggested it needed a proper commentary, mood music and sound effects, possibly with a cartoon-like character to link each image and explain what it was about. In short, the children's imaginations were not captured, which meant any subsequent learning opportunities were lost. The creators are modifying the disc and, our findings suggest, might consider sacrificing some of their undoubtedly good quantity for quality.

A CD which certainly does capture children's imaginations, and deserves the label 'interactive', is Broderbund's *Arthur's Teacher Trouble* (Brown, 1992), developed in the early 1990s and which follows an early 'living book' called *Just Grandma and Me* (Mayer, 1992). Run from a CD, they are, in the company's words, 'stories touched by magic and brought to life with characters and pictures that talk and move and sing and dance'. That's true: the 'pages' are rich in colour and detail, and do come to life when activated by clicking the mouse. The interactive graphics and animation cannot be faulted, but what is more difficult to assess is the educational benefit. The CDs will keep a child amused for long periods, since there is much to explore in each of Arthur's twenty-four pages, but does Broderbund's assertion that 'reading skills are increased through word recognition' hold true?

A group of 10-year-olds who explored the CD were so taken with the animation they largely forgot that the purpose of the book is to read it! Afterwards, they could recount little of the story details, other than the main plot. A lecturer in the university's English department analysed the package and concluded it was important to separate the reading aspects of the story from the animation, as young readers tended to be preoccupied with the moving parts and sound effects rather than plot and character. One candidate for change is the way text on each page is automatically read once to the user before the image is freed for 'clicking'. If the voice were taken off, children would have to read the words for themselves, perhaps obtaining voiced help only when stuck.

Another Broderbund product, *The Playroom* (Grimm et al., 1991), demonstrates the value of obtaining input from children before it is marketed. Designed to encourage young children to think about numbers, letters and time in a 'fun' manner, it has latched on to their innate curiosity to explore and experiment.

One of the activities in *The Playroom* allows children to build up a picture featuring different objects chosen by the child picking a letter. The task develops skills of letter association, phonic skills in relation to the beginnings of words, vocabulary expansion and creativity in building the picture. Younger children are encouraged to tell an adult the story behind their picture. The adult can write this down or record it on audio tape – establishing from an early age the value of words and the meaning they convey. Older children can write their story. Another activity gives pictures representing times of the day, with the user having to put them in the correct order, while a spinner device and a hopscotch game develop number bonds through counting, and can be extended to include simple addition and subtraction.

Other CDs offer the chance for children's creative talents to be stretched, by giving them a stage, the tools and just the right amount of help. *Kid Pix* (Gustaffson et al., 1992; Hickman, 1992), an effective balance of sound and visual effects, was developed to give youngsters a dedicated art program and is a big hit with children. It has also proved popular with the software-related industry, picking up a handful of plaudits and awards in the early 1990s. Children tend to view it as a serious piece of computer kit designed for them, rather than a package adults are sneakily trying to use to teach them something, and so often produce extremely creative work, partly through a greater sense of freedom than they get with other software.

Case Study

> One can learn many things from texts and from blackboards, yet other things are better learned in dynamic visual and acoustic media, especially media that are user controlled. Similarly, some individuals learn well using paper and pencil or from viewing linear movies or other narratives, yet other individuals learn much better from more sensory media – media that incorporate sights and sounds at their core, not simply as decorative facades. (Ambron and Hooper, 1990, p. 14)

As potential 'technology specialists', a recent part of our four-year course involved the examination of a variety of commercial multimedia CDs from an educational perspective. The aim of this exercise was to analyse closely a selected package, look at the likely direction of technological developments and evaluate their implications for the learning environment. We were asked to focus on the contribution that multiple media elements of a program could make to learning outcomes.

We were offered a variety of multimedia materials from which to choose, and after a brief experimentation period on each we selected a program entitled *Le Carnaval des Animaux* (UltraLab, 1994a). This choice was made principally on the basis that on first impressions it seemed 'good'. How then could we be sure that this was truly the case?

Le Carnaval des Animaux is essentially a program which enables the user to explore and interpret the music by Saint-Saëns in a fully interactive way. By controlling the compact disc, the user can explore different parts of the music, annotate selected pieces with audio announcements and 'paint' his/her interpretation to the selections. The creators of the disc say in their accompanying literature:

> This is a stunning and original application to let children explore the imagery in music. It includes many innovative features, including an easy to use drag & drop interface, and

built in support for translation which allows users themselves to produce a version of the software to be used in their own culture, without any need for programming experience. Example translations are included on the disc for Spanish, Catalan and Bulgarian. 'Carnaval' also makes use of the full CD quality audio recording of Saint-Saens' music that is included on the disc.
(UltraLab, 1994a)

We established that the only way successfully to evaluate the multimedia package was by first ascertaining what the creators' overall aims were when designing *Carnaval*. Clearly, a student's work can be accurately marked only when one has a clear understanding of the requirements that he/she was supposed to fulfil.

Having recognized the importance of this insight, we spoke to Stephen Heppell (a member of the *Carnaval* team), who clearly identified three aims of the program:

- first, the program was to be suitable for children with no previous experience of computing and it was also intended to allow for multicultural possibilities;
- second, its purpose was to offer children the freedom to explore the imagery and music by separating it from composition and notation;
- finally, it was hoped that the program would provide children with the confidence to interact easily with multimedia and be able to create something of which they could rightfully be proud.

Having established the overall aims of the program, we were now able to focus on how successfully we felt they were fulfilled.

Having set up the necessary technical equipment, we sat at the computer and began our study, something which initially can only be described as structured play. We observed, hypothesized, tested and evaluated. In short, we experimented. The 'discovery' period allowed us to establish the nature of the multimedia package. So how is *Carnaval* used?

When the program begins the user is greeted by a screen which displays example 'boxes' containing pictures, audio instructions and the music itself. Help is available through the use of 'balloons' but little explanation is required. *Carnaval* incorporates the use of a movable palette which contains all the essential tools.

Creating a personal collection of music and drawings is a straightforward task. A new box is created by dragging the box icon from the control palette to the work area. It is here where the snippets and drawings can be organized. A musical score runs along the bottom of the screen and the music begins when the musical note on the score is clicked upon. The note then begins to 'walk' forward along the score while the user is left to enjoy the corresponding music. It is possible to move the note anywhere along the score, and once a suitable piece of music has been decided upon the user can select it by dragging the chosen piece on to the work area. A musical snippet is thus created.

The pencil icon can then be chosen from the control panel and placed on to the snippet. This takes the user into the painting studio where a range of Hypercard and text tools are waiting to allow the user to interpret his/her selected piece of music graphically.

Our initial interaction with the program was successful. We 'played' with the music and tools, created a new box and even selected snippets of our own to create a personal compilation. However, our feelings of mastery were short-lived. We could not help but feel that the music we created was disappointing. The snippets did not join together how we would have liked, nor were they particularly pleasant to the ear. No, we are not music specialists, but surely we could create something worth listening to.

Feeling extremely disheartened, we decided it was time to sit back from the bright glare of the computer screen and examine what we had actually learned – most of which had been extremely positive.

First, we found the program to be user-friendly and we felt that it would be accessible to even young children with no previous experience of computers. This is fundamentally a result of the neat programming created for the package. The 'drag and drop' control of *Carnaval* makes the software extremely manageable and adds to the simplicity of the interface design. The material's ease of use is clearly of primary importance. No matter how beneficial the learning outcomes may be, if they are inaccessible, they remain hidden away from the learner and as a direct result they are irrelevant and worthless.

Second, we had quickly been able to locate the option to control the language of the computer. This takes the form of a control panel located at the beginning of the program where the user is invited to choose which language messages are to be displayed in. Many classrooms contain children who have expertise in a range of languages. In our opinion, the fact that *Carnaval* supports multiple languages indicates that the creators are aware of the importance of adapting to meet the cultural and specific needs of individual children and reflects the culturally diverse classrooms of today.

Finally, the notation of the music with which we experimented was not a problem – in fact, we had not given it a single thought! The program did not ask us to consider whether a piece of music started with a B^b or an $A^{\#}$. If this had been a necessary requirement, we would both have been extremely deterred from using the package as our feelings of intimidation would have been far too much to bear. We were able to create our own snippets of music using our own musical language which consisted of comments such as 'The next bit needs to be quite high at the beginning' and 'I don't think we should include that squeaky bit!' We discussed pitch, duration, pace and dynamics using our own personal vocabulary which we had brought with us to the computer screen.

We had used the multimedia program with ease, experimented with the tools available and created pieces of music. Perhaps most important of all, we felt in control. What, then, had gone wrong?

Essentially, we were unable to create anything of which we felt proud. The amount of time we spent staring wide-eyed at the disinterested computer screen made little difference – we could not produce anything of value. What we wanted to happen didn't – it was always 'not quite right'.

We mentioned our feelings regarding our lack of ability to one of the program creators. He was keen to point out to us that although we were dissatisfied with our work at the computer, it did not necessarily mean that a child would feel the same way. He advised us to try it out on a child, to be open-minded and not to underestimate children's capabilities.

Following the advice we had been given, we decided to observe a child's first interactions with this multimedia package. For the purpose of this study one child was selected. Shona (aged 10) had limited experience with computers and had no experience of a program such as *Carnaval*.

We initiated our study by simply placing Shona in front of the computer screen. We were careful to explain only a few functional skills such as how to create a new box and a snippet. We made Shona aware of the movable palette, but we did not explain its contents in any detail as we felt that the tools available clearly conveyed their purpose. Having given Shona the minimal amount of information, we left her to her own devices to explore *Carnaval des Animaux*.

We observed Shona while she worked and we felt that the comments she made to herself were interesting and thought-provoking.

> Shona   Mmmm . . . that's interesting! I don't want that bit! That's it! What shall I draw? That bit sounds like people dancing! . . . [sees the light] . . . Oh, I get it!

Although the language used was not technical in nature, it showed that Shona was very deeply involved in her work at the computer. The amount of effort she put into this new learning experience was quite remarkable.

Shona worked happily; then, having experimented with the tools, she explained that she was going to make a 'proper box'. We had spent hours face-to-screen and had as yet been unable to create anything which we felt was worthy of such a title. We were intrigued.

Shona worked for approximately forty-five minutes. She was completely engaged in the task throughout, and the expressions on her face alone told us of the frustration, annoyance, excitement and enjoyment she had experienced.

After what seemed to us a lifetime, Shona announced that she had 'done' her box. We quickly joined her at the computer, overwhelmed with anticipation and eager to see what she had produced. Shona proudly showed us her 'proper' box. All three of us stared at the screen in appreciation of the graphics, text, music, sounds and speech that she had put together.

Quite simply, we were enthralled and very pleased with the end product. Shona had chosen pieces of music and had used her imagination to express her feelings towards these selections. She had created and combined graphics, text, sounds and even her own voice to produce an exciting combination of effects. All three of us felt a great sense of achievement.

So, what had Shona gained from using the program? In our opinion, she had gained a great deal. She had acquired experience of using a computer to achieve desired results and had incorporated many elements of multimedia into a relevant and meaningful activity.

Shona's enthusiasm alone had made the activity worthwhile, but how did her involvement with the program reflect its overall aims? We noted the following points:

- the program had proven to be interesting, exciting and easy to use;
- no previous musical knowledge and understanding was needed to benefit from using the program;
- the program encouraged confidence and offered an opportunity to create something of great satisfaction.

Shona had used the program with ease to create a piece of music which she was delighted to show her work to all and sundry. In no way at all did she feel restricted by her lack of musical understanding. She was challenged, informed and excited. This was made clear to us by the following comment:

Shona   I felt pleased with the music in my box because I am not usually very good at music. I can't tell the difference between a violin and a cello when I hear them but I could make a good piece of music on the computer because I could make the music sound how I wanted it to.

Shona recognized that each snippet of music stood on its own. However, she was still conscious of the fact that the snippets could be linked. She evaluated her work by continually replaying it – thus evaluation became a continuous process.

Shona   I had to keep checking the music because if you have one piece of music that is quite flowing and then you have a piece which is quite jumpy, they might not go well together. I had to keep on checking what I had done or I would have ended up with some really stupid pieces of music.

During her brief experimentation period Shona had developed from apprehensively staring over our shoulders and simply exploring the music and tools which the program contained, to creating and developing her own musical expression and taking her place very securely in the driving seat.

Shona demonstrated that feelings of success were achievable – so where had we gone wrong? We decided that the heart of our frustration lay in the fact that we had been far too concerned with joining the pieces of music and not concerned enough with expressing our feelings towards the individual snippets. We were too fussy and hard to please – fundamentally because we did not know what we wanted ourselves. Consequently, our efforts had resulted in frustration and disappointment. Shona's interaction with the program assured us that by approaching multimedia materials in the most beneficial way, the learning outcomes are greatly improved.

In our opinion *Le Carnaval des Animaux* is an innovatory program as it allows real learning outcomes to take place by offering the learner challenge and pleasure. Perhaps most importantly it recognizes the emergent capabilities of learners and responds to their expectations.

Our study of *Le Carnaval des Animaux* initially began as a technical one. We started out by evaluating the quality of sound, the suitability of graphics and the program's ease of use in general. This led to examining a child's use of the program, and in this way we were able to establish the real capability of the program and so ascertain the true value of sounds, text, graphics and user control.

This study has assured us that the use of multimedia in educational computing is something new and exciting. It brings unique experiences to the learning environment and as a direct result it can dramatically affect the learning which takes place.

We feel that our investigation indicates that learners need to be offered more innovatory software with which to interact so that they can at last be given an opportunity to realize their information potential. Learners should interact, participate, be challenged and be recognized as sophisticated users by the programs they encounter. Active involvement is of paramount importance to their success in learning. In essence, we need more programs which offer innovation and flexibility.

Shona   *Carnaval* was easy to use because you could listen to the music an
                 draw pictures to go with it. I haven't done that on a computer before
                 It is different and exciting and there is nothing really like it.

Our learning in general consists of a whole range of multimedia experiences – wh
should our interaction with a computer be any different?

So what, if anything, has this chapter proved? We hope it has shown that CD-ROM
technology can be educationally beneficial and that it will be playing an increasingl
influential part in classrooms for many years to come. We also trust we have helped t
put a friendlier face on the subject for any readers unsure about this aspect c
information technology. The most important message for serving and would-b
teachers, however, is that the multimedia industry is still in its infancy: teachers hav
the chance to take it by the scruff of the neck and help shape it in a way which will mak
their job easier and more enjoyable, rather than allowing industrialists, designers an
software engineers with a limited knowledge of education simply to present them wit
material which does not do the job. The vast majority of CD-ROM companies are onl
too willing to be guided in what schools need – and we should be ready to tell them in n
uncertain terms! For example, Yorkshire Television and Interactive Learning Prod
ucts, who have formed a partnership to produce educational CD-ROM packages, stat
categorically: 'We are always keen to hear suggestions from teachers for new titles an
improvements that could be made to existing discs. These form a crucial part of ou
continuing development programme.' And Selly Park Girls' School in Birmingham
offers to test commercial titles (Glyn-Jones, 1994), giving it a say, however small, i
shaping the final product which goes on to the market.

The dilemma to which one always returns, however, is one of time. Where does
serving teacher, struggling to keep abreast of growing class sizes, a challenging range c
ability levels, increasing administrative demands and the need to meet the require
ments of the National Curriculum, find the hours to become more technologicall
literate and comfortable, let alone start deciding on the priorities for CD manufac
turers' future output? That's something teachers, heads and governors are now goin
to have to address seriously if we are to play a part, as a profession, in forming our rol
in the schools of tomorrow: time and money spent in looking ahead, formulatin
policies and priorities for information technology and multimedia, will save time
money and heartache later. What's more, and what seems particularly important to u
is that it will enhance the role of the teacher as a communications expert – pushing th
industry to increase the opportunities for relevant, high-quality learning – rather tha
being a lukewarm bit-part actor who unthinkingly speaks the lines the director ha
given him. Our lines are, all too often, written by programmers with little or n
expertise of teaching and learning, although it might be said that: 'The quality c
educational titles is improving as writers extend their understanding of the psycholog
of learning and of children, and discover how to exploit the full potential of th
technology' (Glyn-Jones, 1994). How much better would it be if teachers were pointin
them in the right direction?

Chapter 9

Curriculum Developments
Jon Griffin

It is not many years ago that the computer was thought of as an expensive device suitable only for mathematicians and scientists. Today it is viewed as a necessary piece of household equipment, along with the telephone, hi-fi system, television and video. Indeed, a random survey in any classroom will reveal that most households own a personal computer. For many children, the computer is seen as a games machine, and their interest is in beating their hi-score on the latest game. When in the right hands, the computer is an extremely powerful tool for supporting teaching and learning in both the home and school. In this context parents and teachers have a valuable role to play.

> By the year 2010 the computer will be considered a dinosaur and will be as slow as a tortoise. Personal computers will no longer be operated by hand using a mouse and a keyboard, but will be voice activated. The computer will be as useful as the horse and cart is to modern travel today . . .

Such a statement, by two of my students,[1] hints at the power of the computer of the future and suggests the way that developments will go. Taken in the context of the technological developments over the past fifteen years, it is probably correct and suggests *cheap, fast, extremely powerful*, and *pocket-sized* computers.

Other students in the same group believe that 'in the next century computers will be part of every lesson. Each child will have their *own personal* lap-top computer . . . each lap-top will be logged in to the school's network every morning.' Just as every child now has a calculator as part of their standard school kit, so in the classroom of the future all pupils will also have a pocket computer.

As parents, we should be encouraging our children to use computers for a variety of activities which promote learning. As teachers, we should be embracing this technology, recognizing its weaknesses and strengths and exploiting its potential. In the busy homes and classrooms of today this is not always easy. But, if we don't accept this challenge, then who will? It is our children who will be the losers!

In an earlier chapter, 'Learning Discovery Systems in the Computerized Classroom', I stated that my interest is in how computers affect the way that people think and learn, and declared my belief that computer systems can be developed so that learning can take place as a natural process – I reiterate that belief now!

The past decade has shown a growth in the use of 'content free' programs, such as word processors, databases, spreadsheets, and Logo. It also saw a rise in the use of problem-solving activities. Towards the end of this decade the importance of using information technology in primary schools was highlighted with the introduction of the National Curriculum and further emphasized with the SCAA proposal to separate information technology from design technology. I believe that information technology will transform education in the same way that it has transformed industry and commerce. Indeed, if my students are right, there will be a major and fundamental change by the turn of the century.

There is, however, a significant development and increase in the profile of information technology within the education system. Although dated, figure 9.1 illustrates how information technology permeates the whole curriculum at Key Stages 1 and 2. Furthermore, a close look at the new, draft orders for information technology and the other National Curriculum subjects reveals that in essence this view of information technology remains largely unchanged. It is still about manipulation and communicating, 'in a variety of forms, including combining text, graphics [images] and sound' (SCAA, 1994, p. 3).

The draft orders (SCAA, 1994) move from five themes to two. The new themes are 'communicating and handling information' and 'using IT to investigate'. Further reading of the draft orders reveals that the theme 'using IT to investigate' has two aspects to it, namely 'measurement and control' and 'modelling'. This move simplifies and clarifies the original orders dating from 1990.

The five themes for information technology, listed in figure 9.1 are neatly incorporated into the new orders by:

- combining the themes 'developing ideas and communicating information' and 'information handling' into the theme 'communicating and handling information';
- combining the themes 'modelling' and 'measurement and control' into the theme 'using IT to investigate';
- incorporating the theme 'applications' into both of the new themes.

It is interesting that the new orders take account of the fact that technology is developing at a pace which seems to be 'out of control' and makes technology 'out of date' as soon as it appears in the market-place. However, the importance of information technology is significantly raised by two factors, the first being that 'IT and D&T should be presented separately, . . . , and that IT should be separated from D&T for assessment and reporting purposes' (SCAA, 1994, p. iii), the second that 'teachers of all subjects [will] have separate copies of the IT requirements' (p.iii). In effect, this means that the cross-curricular nature of information technology, highlighted in figure 9.1, will continue – the activities will remain the same, while the attainment targets and programmes of study references will change.

With the advent of the microcomputer in the late 1970s there has been a significant growth in the amount of computer activity being done at all levels within our schools. This activity has two foci, one being as a subject of study for which some 100,000 candidates sit examinations each year (DES, 1990a), the other being as a cross

Theme	Information Technology	English	Mathematics	Science	Design Technology	Geography	History
Developing ideas and communicating information	5.1 using computer 5.2 pictures, words and symbols 5.3 drafting 5.4 retrieve, develop, organize and present 5.5 present for purposes	3.3 drafting 3.4 redrafting 3.5 editing	11.2 angles, logo 11.3 logo, function machines 7.4 coordinates PROC 11.4 coordinates maps 5.5 logo	12.2 communication 12.3 store information	2.4 record ideas 2.5 record progress of ideas		
Information handling	5.2 pictures, words and symbols 5.3 database 5.4 information retrieval		12.3 use database 12.4 interrogate database 12.5 create and interrogate database	12.3 select text, number, sound, graphics	1.4 devise ways of gathering information	1.2 weather data 2.2 data collection 1.4 weather data 3.4 weather data 3.5 weather data	3.3 database census
Modelling	5.5 form and test hypotheses				2.3 use models 2.4 resources requirements	1.3 use of coordinates	
Measurement and control	5.3 control 5.4 logo 5.5 control			12.4 detect and measure environmental changes, micro electronics 12.5 logic gates 1.5 measuring instruments	2.3 use models 3.4 use ... to assist making	1.4 weather	
Applications	5.3 describe and compare 5.4 question and everyday applications 5.5 data on computers						

Figure 9.1 *Information technology across the curriculum to satisfy the requirements of the 'original' National Curriculum.*

curricular tool in which the computer is used to support and enhance learning across a range of subjects and across the complete age range.

It is therefore not surprising that the use of information technology features within teacher training courses and that the Council for the Accreditation of Teacher Education has raised the profile of information technology by insisting that all courses which prepare students for a career in teaching must contain an element of information technology within them. Indeed, the requirement is that

On completion of their course, all students should be able to select and make appropriate use of a range of equipment and resources to promote learning. In particular, all courses should contain compulsory and clearly identifiable elements which enable students to make effective use of information technology in the classroom and provide a sound basis for their subsequent development in this field. They should be able to:

- make confident personal use of a range of software packages and information technology devices appropriate to their subject specialism and age range;
- review critically the relevance of software packages and information technology devices to their subject specialism and age range and judge the potential value of these in classroom use;
- make constructive use of information technology in their teaching and in particular prepare and put into effect schemes of work incorporating appropriate uses of information technology;
- evaluate the ways in which the use of information technology changes the nature of teaching and learning.

(Anglia Polytechnic University, 1991 pp. 10–11)

This requirement, combined with the National Curriculum requirement that a pupils be able to manipulate text, graphics and sound, brings an exciting ne dimension to information technology as the possibilities for developing interactiv multimedia systems for use in our classrooms are opened up by the advent of powerft modern computers able to control text, graphics, sound and video with relative eas and at a low cost.

Interactive multimedia is an exciting area within which researchers and others hav been developing systems suitable for use in teacher education and in primary schoc classrooms. Leaders in this field include Ambron (Apple Computer, USA) an Heppell (Anglia Polytechnic University, England). Although the extension of the work into schools can be clearly seen, the focus of their work has been very much at a academic level and aimed at researchers, higher education, and the corporate market

There is clearly a requirement that all student teachers receive a basic course i information technology covering word processing, databases, spreadsheets, logc control technology, desk-top publishing, classroom management and organization and the requirements of the National Curriculum. At Anglia Polytechnic University w provide courses for all primary students in years one, two, and three of the BEd cours (see figure 9.2) – full course notes are incorporated on the *Insights for Teachers an Parents* CD (UltraLab, 1994).

In addition, there is a need for well-educated specialists with both understanding an flexibility in the use of information technology in society, government, commerce industry, and within the education system. In addressing this need within teache training, I have developed a number of courses for student teachers. This has resulte in changes to the curriculum for students on teacher training courses, and in its turn ha required that teacher educators gain insights into the effects of new technologies an delivery systems, and competencies in the use of these technologies.

Preliminary research into what has been written about the effects of new technolc gies and delivery systems in teacher education shows that little relevant literature i available. It is not difficult to speculate why this might be the case. It might reflect th emergence of this area as a new topic for research and also the lack of awareness withi the teaching profession, and particularly with teacher educators, of the potential fc the use of 'new technologies' within the teaching and learning situations. It migh further reflect the fact that the recent innovations in information technology that hav enabled powerful computers and the associated software to be produced at a low cos are too recent to have allowed for research in schools and universities to be carried out

COURSE OUTLINE	
SESSION	**CONTENT**
1	**Computers in the Classroom** What skills and knowledge do you bring to this area of work, how do we use computers in the classroom, and why?
2	**Creative Writing with the Computer** Word processing: what does it mean for learning?
3	**Control over the Computer** Logo, programming, wheels for the mind.
4	**Computers in the Classroom** Classroom organization, management, assessment, the effect of home computing on learning.
5	**Classifying and Categorizing** Using and designing databases, organizing database work.
6	**Modelling and Calculating** Spreadsheets: modelling finances, recipes, and experiments with numbers.
7	**Clinic** Investigating task-specific software, extending your knowledge of the basics, responding to individual student needs.
8, 9, and 10	**Control Technology** Making simple models, using the computer to control a sequence of events carried out by the model.
11, 12, and 13	**Desktop Publishing** The design and production process of a range of documents.

Figure 9.2 *Outline of the information technology course for all BEd students.*

t also reflects the fact that teachers have not yet had opportunities to either use this echnology or to appreciate its true potential.

For the wider issue involving the *use* of computers in education, much time and effort as been expended in researching word processing, desktop publishing, Logo, and other topics. Time has also been spent researching and developing multimedia systems t an academic level for use by researchers, higher education, and the corporate market. Thus, it is worth taking some time to review the work of others in this area.

The Multimedia Revolution

> Revolution and evolution are recurring themes in the . . . computing world . . . In the course of the Macintosh evolution came another revolution – this one from the brilliant mind of . . . Bill Atkinson. As long as I've known Bill, he has had a passion for empowering people with new tools that extend the mind's reach. His efforts in this area . . . culminated in a revolution known as HyperCard . . . In parallel with HyperCard's ready accessibility came increased interest in multimedia. HyperCard quickly became the software platform of choice for creative artists who mixed on-screen animation, digitised and pre-recorded compact disc audio, and live motion video into richly woven experiences for education and personal enrichment.
> (Goodman, 1990, p. xix)

HyperCard is an enabler for interactive applications and has the potential for bringing this technology into every primary classroom in a way that puts the learner at the centre of the technology and in control of it, rather than being just a passive user. A useful definition says that

> 'interactive multimedia' . . . is a collection of computer centred technologies that give a user the capability to access and manipulate text, sounds, and images. Just as word processing programs today enable users to integrate text and graphics, multimedia programs in the near future will enable users to access not only libraries of text documents but also storehouses of music, sound effects, speech, still images, animation, and movies. In addition, multimedia users will be able to manipulate this lexicon of material and add their own material.
> (Ambron and Hooper, 1990, p. xi)

Hooper looks at HyperCard from a pedagogical viewpoint and gives the reader insights into teaching and learning processes. She shares my view that 'the pedagogical arguments [are] the most exciting to convey' (Ambron and Hooper, 1990, p. 11).

Ambron and Hooper's book *Learning with Interactive Multimedia* (1990) introduces a range of contributors from schools who share their experiences with this technology. Nicol (1990) introduces the notion of a continuum in which children at one extreme are passive users of HyperCard and rely on others to provide the material and context for its use while at the other end of the continuum they are in control and use HyperCard to develop their own material and thus have control over the creation and presentation of material (p. 145).

Mintz (1990) sees HyperCard being used in a number of ways within the school system, two of which are 'by the teacher for the children' and 'by the children for the children' (p. 157). He envisages both teacher and student setting up learning situations and using interactive multimedia presentations for the communication of information. Mintz sees HyperCard as 'an incredible tool in the hands of users who are willing to understand and use it and an awe-inspiring tool for teachers who have the time, willingness, and ability to use it with and for children' (p. 158).

Collins and Lengel (1990) address the reality of the use of HyperCard and multimedia techniques within education. They note that computers, and indeed HyperCard, are used for 'instructional' or 'drill and practice' programs. This is hardly the most advanced use of the medium, for which they give some explanation:

> We must remember that schools move slowly in adopting computer technology . . . [and they] . . . go through a common series of developmental stages in their use of this technology:

- The P Stage: Schools teach Programming and treat the computer as an object of instruction. At this stage, the computer is a Peculiar item in the school, usually a Personal item 'belonging' to one or two teachers who brought it into the school.
- The D stage: Schools use computers for Drill and practice in the regular curricular Disciplines, especially in mathematics and reading. Computers are Diffused throughout the school. Disappointment often results when the promised 'computer revolution' fails to materialise.
- The T stage: Schools use computers as productivity Tools, Tailored to the needs of students, Teachers, and the curriculum. Schools move away from direct instruction with computers and toward the use of general tools such as word processing, databases, spreadsheets, and Telecommunications.

(pp. 195–6)

Although many schools will recognize the D stage, there are significant numbers of them which are entering the T stage. Collins and Lengel (1990) propose that the next stage will include interactive multimedia (p. 196). And, although this is a long way off for many schools, there is a need to investigate this area so that we will be ready when the time comes. Indeed, institutions involved in the preparation of teachers at an undergraduate level have a special responsibility, especially as a student entering university in 1992 on a four-year Bachelor of Education programme will not be entering the job market as a qualified teacher until September 1996.

Cincinnati County Day School (Ohio, USA) is one in which the use of computer technology is at an advanced stage. Indeed, it is beyond the T stage and has fully embraced the use of HyperCard and multimedia systems. Hofmeister (1990) reports on and gives examples of work by teachers and students. The innovations at this school provide a useful model for other schools in the use of powerful modern computers for a range of applications, including the use of interactive multimedia systems for teaching and learning. Stebbins (1990) also reports on the activities at West High School in Columbus, Ohio. Most examples of the use of these technologies are found in secondary schools and usually relate to a specific subject area – Stebbins' work is science-based. Campbell and Hanlon (1990) address issues of resourcing, equipment, the design and production of learning materials, and methodologies for teaching with HyperCard in the classroom. Like the other examples above, their work is based in secondary schools.

In all the above case studies the learner as well as the teacher was involved in the production of learning materials. Students were not just passive learners, but very much active participants in their own learning.

> The real question is whether multimedia can deliver true meaning without conscious interaction. One way of achieving conscious interaction without disturbing engagement is by considering the learner as author and emerging hypermedia systems appear to be taking due note of this issue. To come clean, there is very little data supporting the concept of authoring as an effective learning tool. Experience with 'Intermedia' might reasonably suggest that such a system promotes effective learning in so far as users [learners] are engaged actively in making their own connections and integration at the conceptual level. (Barker and Tucker, 1990, p. 150)

In leading the way forward, Stephen Heppell has found backing to set up a 'centre of excellence' known as the UltraLab at Anglia Polytechnic University. The main focus of his work is to bring to the attention of academics, researchers, commerce, industry and government the impact and importance of 'new technologies and delivery systems' on teaching and learning. As he says,

at the 'Information Technology in the Learning Environment' [UltraLab] unit here at Anglia we are working to develop Multimedia tools for the primary classroom, appropriate staff development strategies, and the summative and formative advice frameworks that are needed alongside them. We are working particularly at repairing the fractured interface between primary and secondary phase education. For example, by giving primary children simple intuitive tools that allow them to author presentations of their text and graphics, mixed with others' video images, or high quality music sounds, we have been delighted (and not a little surprised) by the quality of work produced at this early exploratory stage and the opportunities it offers for progression.
(Heppell, quoted in Fields, 1990)

I also agree with Heppell's view that

Primary schools have barely begun the process of integrating the computer successfully into the everyday processes of learning in the primary classroom. Before this challenge is fully met they are facing a significant leap forward in technology and the potential learning environment that it can resource. The challenge comes from multimedia – the powerful integration of text, graphics, sound, animation, and video under computer control.
(Heppell, 1990)

The challenge is exciting, and it is extremely useful to have such ready access to a un like Heppell's UltraLab, in order to be able to see the latest technologies, share idea: and collaborate on research in this important area.

There is now a growing body of knowledge being developed around HyperCard an multimedia systems, a body of knowledge based on a wide range of uses an applications, of which teacher education is one. Throughout all these application there seems to be a consensus that HyperCard and multimedia systems 'serve as framework for learning. The HyperCard structure actually mimics some of ou thinking processes. For one thing, it tends to involve manipulating bite-sized pieces c information – a graphic, a sound, an image' (Sempor, 1990, p. 56).

After assimilating the ideas outlined above, I felt that it was important for me to tr out my own ideas. In doing so, my study attempted to encapsulate the ideas of Winte on 'action research', in that

its use and even its awkwardness serve to conjure forth that most intractable of questions for social science: what is the relationship between theoretical and practical knowledge? The question concerns not only the nature of knowledge itself, but the relationship between the various knowledge producing institutions, ranging from the university to the workplace. The specific form of the question . . . concerns integration: how can theory be more integrated with practice [and vice versa]; how can education be more closely integrated with work [and vice versa]; how can research be more closely integrated with action [and vice versa]? . . . 'Action-research', then is a phrase used to invoke the desirability of closing these separations, [and] of enriching these impoverishments.
(Winter, 1987, p. vii).

It was of paramount importance to me to be able to design, plan, implement an evaluate a course that enabled the students to experience the concepts, ideas an opportunities that modern technologies present to teaching and learning. I could no however, forget the students' basic need to gain confidence and expertise in doing th simplest of things on a computer. The monitoring and evaluating of these activities len themselves to research, and in particular to the ideas of Winter, expressed above. Suc questions as 'How can theory be more integrated with practice?', 'How can educatio be more closely integrated with work?' and 'How can research be more closel integrated with action?' take on real meaning. In particular, I needed to be able to (an indeed did) review a range of curriculum proposals before coming up with and implementing a particular course proposal. Having used my professional judgement in the creation of a course, I needed to be able to evaluate it. In order to achieve this I used three tools. The first of these was a questionnaire, the second an evaluation of the sessions, and the third the use of student interviews. The questionnaire was administered at the start and end of the course and was devised in order to give me feedback on a whole range of issues including student attitudes and experiences and to assist in the process of evaluating the effectiveness of the course.

The remainder of this chapter provides a case study of a curriculum development which I carried out in order to formulate my own views and to have first-hand experience of this new and exciting area of work. The target group in this case were third-year primary BEd students who were all taking English as their main subject. Since carrying out this study I have been involved in a range of innovations – one of which is outlined in Chapter 8 by Hales and Russell.

The monitoring of the sessions involved a form of 'triangulation' which used myself, an audio record of each session, and photographs and video material to evaluate the sessions and the course. By taking some trouble over the evaluation, I acquired significant insights into student reactions to individual components of the course and was able to consider the 'teaching and learning' that took place.

Within the study the students were interviewed to collect 'information in a form which permits the answers from each subject to be put together to give an accurate picture' (Nisbet, 1970, p. 32). These were 'unstandardized' interviews in that they allowed a series of questions to be asked depending on the responses and cues given by individual students. They also gave students greater freedom to make an input to the evaluation process.

Case Study

'Computers in Language and Literature': insights into new technologies and delivery systems in teacher education for Year 3 BEd students, who are taking English as their main subject. (This case study is presented on a week-by-week basis.)

Figure 9.3 provides a summary of the course outline that the students undertook.

Week One

The first week was used to administer a 'pre-course' questionnaire. It also enabled an introduction to be given to the course which set the scene for the work to be covered and provided some insights into the use of technology in 'teaching and learning'. As one student said:

Marion: I didn't know a computer could do all those things.

And, as she also reflected:

Marion: I will never be able to do this!

This sentiment was echoed by many of the students in the group. I gave an assurance to them that they would be able to do these things.

SCHEDULE OF SESSIONS	
WEEK	**CONTENT**
1	• Complete 'pre-course' questionnaire • Keynote presentation to introduce the nature and scope of the course and to provide insights into information technology within education
2	• Writing and word processing in the primary classroom • Special devices (for example, the concept keyboards)
3	• Understanding computers ... • Content-free software ...
4	• Understanding computers ... • The use of adventure games in 'language and literature'
5	• Introduction to the Apple computer • Microsoft Works (word processing)
6	• Introduction to HyperCard (Vincent, Talking Book, and Work Rooms).
7	• Text, images, and sound in HyperCard • 'Fields' and 'buttons' in HyperCard
8 and 9	• HyperCard project: creating a 'talking book'
10	• Synthesis and prognostication • Complete 'post-course' questionnaire

Figure 9.3   *Outline for the course 'Computers in Language and Literature'.*

By looking at the responses to question E1 (see figure 9.4) on the pre-cours
questionnaire, we can see that 11 students felt unable to load and run a program, whil
only one student considered herself to be an expert at this activity. The mean respons
to question E1 was 2.4 – suggesting a moderately low level of competence. When i
came to preparing disks (E2 in figure 9.4) and copying disks (E3 in figure 9.4) th
responses show even less competence at these activities, with 19 out of 32 being unabl
to prepare a disk and 17 out of 32 being unable to copy a disk, and in both cases none o
them considered themself to be an expert. The mean responses for questions E2 and E
were 1.78 and 1.9 respectively. In this graph category 1 is where the respondent i
unable to do the activity and category 5 is where the respondent is an expert.

The keynote presentation was a multimedia presentation based on principles an
concepts enshrined within the National Curriculum. This presentation gave a contex
and put substance on the demands of the National Curriculum in areas such as th
manipulation of text, sound and images. The presentation proposed the notion that it i
an exciting time in educational computing and introduced the students to a range o

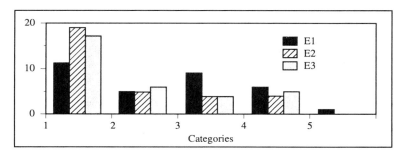

Figure 9.4 *Bar chart of the ability of students to load and run a computer programme (E1), format a disc (E2) and copy disks (E3).*

ural, visual and textual environments. These environments included childrens' voices, sound effects, audio compact discs, graphics, video disks, recorded video on computer disc, text, and combinations of these and other effects. At the conclusion of the presentation I suggested that

> we will have to educate a population to think creatively, productively, and prolifically. To adequately prepare a generation for this technology based information age, we must foster a positive predisposition toward learning. The best entry point for beginning this techno-logical education is with the very young child, . . . one way of doing this is through effective applications of technology.
> (Jenkins, 1990, p. 113)

Week Two

Week two addressed the issue of providing the students with the necessary skills, confidence and insights for using word processors in primary classrooms.

> A wordprocessor is a computer program that serves as a versatile writing aid with many powerful editing tools. A person can insert or delete words and sentences, rearrange paragraphs, or locate and replace misspelled words quickly and easily. Some sophisticated word processing programs can even detect common grammatical or stylistic problems . . . When reading instruction is computer based, teachers can use word processing operations to build connections between the acts of reading and writing.
> (Geoffrion and Geoffrion, 1983, p. 10)

The word processor used during this session was a program called Folio (Tediman Software, 1988). Folio is a simple word processor which can be found in all of the schools in the area surrounding Anglia Polytechnic University – it is now being replaced by Pendown (Hunter, 1992), and in due course this too will be replaced. It is so the one that students are likely to encounter during their school-based work. Although it is very limiting and does not have the sort of facilities mentioned earlier such as spell, grammar, and style checkers, it does, however, have the ability to be connected to a concept keyboard, thus making it possible for pre-readers, young children and slow learners to be able to produce high-quality material with relative ease. The students soon became engrossed in using Folio and expressed enthusiasm about using it and other programs in school.

As the session progressed the students gained in confidence and acquired t
necessary skills to use Folio. At times the students' technical vocabulary let them dow
but this did not stop them from assimilating Folio for themselves as a precursor
adapting it for use in schools with children.

> *Michelle:*   . . . we need to use this [pause as she tries to think of the word] 'b
> and 'bob' [meaning the printer] . . .

A few moments later:
> *Shirley:*   We should save first.
> *Sarah:*   Yes, save it!
> *Shirley:*   [short pause while they save their work] Now we can print . . .

They sequenced their thoughts and actions automatically, saved their work a
printed it out in an appropriate format, having 'taken on board' that the work could
lost if anything went wrong in the printing process. By this time the students were
complete control:

> *Dr Griffin:*   . . . has everyone got some text in . . . changed its . . . size . . . sha
> . . . format?

There were nods of assent all round, Michelle asserted herself, Sarah compliment
Michelle, and Jonathan raised a quick query:

> *Michelle:*   Yes! Really!
> *Sarah:*   Oh! that's lovely Michelle.
> *Jonathan:*   We've got double spacing.
> *Dr Griffin:*   That's because you've chosen a large font. [pauses to check th
> Jonathan understands, then continues] . . . look, you've certainly g
> enough text in . . . this is not about typing text, it's about changing
> shape, size and its format . . . Now note that one of the facilities th
> you have not got is a spell checker . . .

At this point there was a brief discussion about spell checkers and other faciliti
offered on modern word processors before introducing the concept keyboard. Th
concept keyboard is a device that enables one to enter information into the comput
It can be used in addition or as an alternative to the standard QWERTY keyboard. Th
concept keyboard is a device which is used with overlays. These overlays can ha
words printed on them, or have pictures, or indeed have both words and pictures
them. Originally the concept keyboard was created for use by children with learni
disabilities, but its use by the younger child and 'pre-reader' was quickly recogniz
and today it is most commonly found in the infant classroom. Its strength is that it
easily programmed for use with a word processor to enter a word, phrase, sentence
short paragraph at a single press of the concept keyboard, thus enabling a child
create sophisticated pieces of work which give them a sense of pride and satisfactio
The printed material can also be used for reading by the child.

At this time the students showed a lack of confidence in their ability to carry out th
tasks required to create an overlay for use with children. This lack of confiden
showed particularly as they were (successfully) completing the activity:

> *Jonathan:*   Press return [pause] . . . you press it then press return . . . Ooh!

Cheryl:	Oh! What have you done to it?
Jonathan:	[following some activity] What are you doing?
Shirley:	I'm trying to get this to work. By pressing that it should reveal the boxes, but . . . [realizes that it does reveal the boxes] Oh, look it does!

By the end of the session the students had begun to gain in confidence, they could also see the potential of using the concept keyboard in the classroom, and a number of them made arrangements to borrow a concept keyboard to take into schools for use with children during their school-based activities.

Week Three

On looking at the responses to the questionnaire, I noted that 23 out of the 32 students indicated that they wanted to know more about how the computer worked (see figure 9.5). I also noted that the responses to questions E1, E2 and E3 (see figure 9.4) indicated that the students were unable to do such basic things as load and run a program, prepare a disk, and copy a disk. Thus I felt it essential to respond to this need by incorporating time into each session in order to develop these basic skills and give, at a 'low level', the students some understanding of how a computer works.

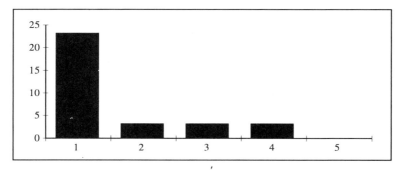

Figure 9.5 *Bar chart showing the student need to know more about the computer (1 = need to know; 5 = don't need to know; 2, 3, and 4 = somewhere in between).*

In responding to this need I used the analogy of a secretary at work to describe the components and processes of a computer. In the analogy, the secretary's 'in-tray' represented the computer's input device; the secretary's 'out-tray' represented the computer's output device; the secretary while working represented the processes going on within the computer; and the filing cabinet represented the computer's storage device. The analogy was extended to look at the type of work that secretaries commonly do, namely, typing and filing, and how this work parallels the work most commonly done by children on computers in schools, namely word processing and information-handling – activities which also form a major part of the National Curriculum for information technology.

I also addressed the issue of preparing and copying disks – something that I came back to on a number of subsequent sessions.

The second half of the session was given over to looking at content-free software and in particular to a language program called Tray. Like all content-free software Tray enables the teacher or the learner to decide and control the nature and content of the text, thus making it relevant to the learner and to the topic being studied. This program encouraged the students to collaborate and discuss their work:

Jonathan:	Ah! this is it . . . no probs! What is it [referring to the text] about?
Sarah:	It's about [thinks] a 'surprise and delighted' . . . [laughs as she realizes that at this stage she doesn't know] . . .
Sarah:	'on first' [as she works out a section of text] . . . [pauses] . . . We are receiving all these 'e's'.
Jonathan:	[repeats Sarah] We're finding lots of 'e's'.
Cheryl:	[interjects with] 'on first', 'on first'! [as she works out another piece of text]
Jonathan:	'on first' [as he appreciates Cheryl's contribution] . . .

The discussion continued until much later, when they had inserted a great deal more text. They then concluded that it was about an 'underwater garden'. There was a noticeable increase in the students' confidence by the end of the session. It was also difficult to prise them away from the computers.

Sarah:	Oh! Yes! [they all laugh]
Dr Griffin:	[there was a noticeable bit of excitement] What did you just get?
Sarah:	[with confidence] It works, it's easy.
Dr Griffin:	Let us stop here.
Cheryl:	Can't we finish to see what it says . . .

And, of course we looked at the completed text.

Week Four

The fourth week saw the conclusion of the activities on the BBC computer, a computer which although outdated (1970s technology) is commonly found in schools at both primary and secondary levels – these are now being replaced by a range of computers including Archimedes, Apples, IBMs, and Nimbuses. The activities in the first four weeks had addressed the issues of developing technical skills and looking at information technology as this technology applies to today's classrooms.

The emphasis of the fourth week was to look at adventure games and their place in the primary curriculum. The students got a great deal out of the session and were particularly keen on the collaboration and language work that evolved from using adventure programs. In addition to concentrating on adventure games, one of the groups witnessed me give an introduction to the session in which everything went wrong. Within ten minutes of starting, the first computer 'played up' and became unusable due to a screen failure; this was then followed by every computer that I used failing to operate. As a consequence I had to spend a few moments making up a system which would work by using bits from different computers.

This is a serious problem that faces many teachers in the classroom! It is made more serious by the fact that the teachers do not have expertise or experience from which to sort out the technological problems that arise. I therefore took the opportunity to concentrate on the issue and asked the students what they would do on occasions like this, when 'nothing goes right'.

> *Dr Griffin:* We've had a short go with the adventure games, but not as long as I would have intended, but we got a flavour . . . I think it is appropriate because of the disaster at the beginning to actually talk about that at this point and get some feedback . . . but it happens to teachers in the classroom and it is a major contributing factor – I think – to why teachers do not use technology.
>
> *Michelle:* If your supervisor comes in you don't want these things [computers] messing you about and making you look stupid, especially if it was someone like you. Initially anyway.
>
> *Dr Griffin:* Actually, you would be better off if it was someone like me – I would understand and be able to help.

The discussion continued to focus around feelings of inadequacy and being unable to cope, and the students showed the classic signs which I have described elsewhere, when all of us from time to time have learning difficulties and we, as otherwise intelligent people, have been made to feel like 'idiots' by the simplest of problems. An example of this is the inability of adults to use computers, an effect caused by computer phobia. Other examples include the inability of many people to do mathematics or learn a foreign language for no apparent reason.

The students finally concluded that what was needed was more courses, such as this, within initial teacher education and for practising teachers. They also commented on the need for each classroom to have a computer and finally, as one student said:

> *Sarah:* You just need to take time to have a go.

Thus, a session that started off with a major disaster had a provided a useful teaching point and had a positive effect on the students. I think, on the quiet, they were quite delighted to see me having problems!

Week Five

This session allowed the students to develop their word-processing skills at their own level by using more powerful computers and word-processing packages than are currently used in schools. They used Microsoft Works on the Apple Macintosh. Microsoft Works is an 'integrated' package which includes a word-processor, database, spreadsheet and communications facilities. In addition to using Works to create text, insert and delete words and sentences, rearrange paragraphs, and locate and replace misspelled words, the students also looked at issues of typeface and page design and layout as an introduction to using HyperCard for producing a 'talking book'. The most difficult thing that the students found with using the Apple computer was controlling the mouse – they found their co-ordination was poor and they struggled with 'pointing' and 'dragging'.

The students were clearly gaining in confidence and expertise and were regularly seen in the open-access facilities trying out the programs that had been used in the sessions as well as coming across problems that required 'new' software. The student were beginning to fulfil Piaget's notions of 'assimilation and adaption' (McNally, 1974)

Week Six

This was the point when the students began to look seriously at issues relating to new technologies and delivery systems in education. I introduced the session by showing them three HyperCard-based applications.

The first, 'Vincent' (Jek and Voon, 1990), presented the paintings of Vincent van Gogh together with the words and music of Don McClean. The second, 'Work Room (Heppell et al., 1991), is a package for primary children which allows a range of activities to be carried out in 'workrooms', activities which are 'commonly found in learning environments all over the world: story writing, spelling, calculator puzzles data collection and handling' (Heppell and Millwood, 1992, p. 4). The philosophy underpinning the 'workrooms' is clearly expressed by Heppell when she says:

> We have also tried to recognise the way that learning takes place in real classrooms and real homes. For example, in most of the workrooms the user can stop at any time and leave the computer for another activity but their work will be automatically saved and indexed so that they can return to it later.
> (Heppell and Millwood, 1992, p. 4)

The third application was to look at a 'talking book' produced by other students. The 'talking book' enabled the students to focus in on the area that they had to develop. enabled them to address issues relating to presenting learning material – issues which affect readability, meaning and imagery by the use of text, sound and graphics.

Week Seven

> Teaching . . . and learning have traditionally been people oriented activities. Therefore any discussion of the pedagogical applications of computers should take into account the basic nature of human communication. Humans are naturally multi-channel communic-ators. That is they use a number of communication channels [often simultaneously] to get across and receive messages.
> (Barker, 1989, p. 32)

Thus the focus of week seven was to look at HyperCard as a medium for integrating text, images and sound. In order to do this the students worked with cards, fields and buttons within HyperCard. The fields contained text and buttons which could activate sequence of events, such as moving from one card to another or playing a pre-recorded sound. The cards contained these fields, buttons and images in a coherent way to portray the information that the students wished to communicate. Thus, with the advent of powerful modern computers and authoring packages such as HyperCard, we now have the capability to emulate the channels available to humans. By integrating text, images and sound with a computer the students were able to create an interactive multimedia system which consisted of multiple communication channels.

I started the session by raising these issues and demonstrating to the students how to create a stack, cards, fields and buttons. In addition I showed the students how to enter text, sound and images. The students were then given time to practise these skills and to experiment with HyperCard.

By this stage of the course the students were reasonably autonomous in working at the computer. Although they still lacked many skills, they were beginning to have the confidence to try things out, make mistakes, learn from these mistakes, and achieve worthwhile results. By the end of the session all the students had created a stack with a number of cards which incorporated fields, buttons, text, sound and images. And, as Jonathan said to Michelle:

Jonathan: I'll leave it in your capable hands.

A remark which could have applied to any of the students.

Weeks Eight and Nine

For these two weeks the students were set the task of producing a piece of material which was relevant to the age range for which they were preparing to teach. The learning material had to be developed in HyperCard and had to involve text, images and sound in an integrated way. The students were also given the opportunity to complete the tasks in a time of their choosing or in the time allocated for teaching. Many of the students elected to choose the time in which they completed the work. As the students developed computer-based learning material (a talking book) they really began to appreciate the power and potential of powerful modern computers and the relative ease with which the talking book was developed. The time available did not really allow the students the time to develop all of the skills to become totally autonomous, but it did allow them to gain valuable insights into the potential of new technologies and delivery systems for the learning environment. Indeed, another student echoed Marion's comment from week one as she began to appreciate and gain insights into the potential that computers had for learning:

Michelle: I didn't appreciate that they [computers] could do these things . . .

She then went further than Marion had done in her earlier conversation, by saying:

Michelle: . . . so easily . . .

All the students completed at least one page of material containing the three elements of text, images and sound. Some were able to do this without any assistance, while others needed a great deal of help. But, in view of the shortness of the course both they and I were extremely pleased with their efforts. I joined the individual pages produced by the students into a coherent package (a talking book).

Week Ten

Week ten was the last week of the course and consisted of three items. The first was that the students looked at the compilation of their work. This enabled them to see their work as a finished product and gave them the opportunity to see each other's work. The second item was to complete the post-course questionnaire. The third aspect was to discuss the course. The students' comments were interesting and can be put into four categories. Namely, comments referring to the timing of the course, comments referring to the duration of computer courses, comments referring to the format of the course, and, finally, comments referring to the effect of this course on their attitude towards computers. Many of the students also wrote their own comments under section E of the questionnaire. Listed below are a selection of the students' responses which reflect the consensus of opinion.

Timing of the Course

Julie: I think that this course should be earlier in our main course. Possibly . . . at the end of the first year . . .

Duration of Computer Courses

Helen: I need more time on computers . . .

Angela: I really would have appreciated more time . . . and perhaps some practical experience . . . supervised . . . in schools.

Alison: Nowhere near enough time allocated to computers in the four-year course.

Ivy: For a four-year course the contact with computers has been too short . . .

Format of the Course

Two students specifically raised the issue of the duration and intensity of the course:

Jacqui: I would have liked [the] course to be more intensive . . . I feel as if we have only scratched the surface [Which we have!] . . . the course should be followed up with further computer work in year four.

Chris: A daily [intensive] course would have been more beneficial . . . to reinforce learning, with much more college time spent on computer learning . . .

The Effect of this Course on Student Attitudes

A large number of students commented on their increased confidence as a result of this course. Their responses are summarized below:

Marion: [Remember her saying that she would never be able to do anything on a computer] I feel I have a more positive attitude and am not afraid of computers any more . . .

Gillian: I have enjoyed working with the computer this term. I have been able to use a program for my project work [she is not the only one who now uses computers to aid their own learning and childrens' learning] . . .

Chris:	It has helped my confidence greatly . . .
Lyn:	I feel slightly more competent. What I really need is a lot of practical experience [she is right – the hard work is only just beginning] . . .
Michelle:	This course has helped me to become more confident when using computers . . . I am not scared of them anymore!

This feedback was extremely encouraging, and suggested that the course design, content and delivery was on the right lines. It also gave insights for modifying the overall provision of computing within the four-year degree programme, and as a consequence the programme spanning years one, two and three (see figure 9.2) was devised and is now running. In addition, a range of courses for mathematics, English and other main subjects has been devised, along with the introduction of a main course in technology. From such a small innovation much has materialized. We live in hope, as three of my first-year students said to me:

Fifteen years from now computers will be a part of everyone's everyday life from a very early age. In primary schools, teachers *will* use the computer, . . . the blackboard, chalk and chalk dust will only be talked about on history databases . . .

NOTE

1. Comments from the following students have been included in this chapter: Glynis Armitage, Teresa Thompson, Karen Cole, Jill Field, Caroline Britain, Samantha Jolley and Tracy Smith (first-year student teachers, Anglia Polytechnic University, 1994).

Chapter 10

The New Millennium and the Future of Learning[1]

Stephen Heppell

It is easy to speculate about the future. Sadly, however, that ease of prognostication is rarely matched by accuracy. This is especially true in the domains of technology and of learning. Indeed, the 'history of the future' is littered with the wreckage of apparently clear extrapolation, and of those who set sail in certainty on the basis of it. We may characterize this inaccuracy by suggesting that, where pedagogic change is anticipated, the pace of change always disappoints, while, when technology is involved, the pace of change is consistently underestimated.

Either way, we can always be relied on to misjudge the pace of change. Worse still, if the accurate prediction of the pace of change is elusive, the substance of change is even harder to anticipate. With technology, it seems that even in circumstances where individuals are closely identified with the origination of a particular development they are rarely able to anticipate the impact that it will make. The telephone offers us a good example.

When Alexander Graham Bell was developing telephone technology, his papers suggest that he thought he was developing something akin to today's radio; he anticipated families gathering round the phone to hear music, Sunday sermons, drama or weather forecasts, or to enjoy listening in on important public speeches. Indeed Telephon Hiromondu in Budapest actually operated until the early 1920s with just such a system: novels and plays, share prices, weather and debates were all broadcast down the phone lines, for communal listening. Bell was wrong, though; for most of this century the phone functioned as a very synchronous, personal and symmetrical information system. Paradoxically, recent changes in compression technology have seen Bell's original vision belatedly start to become true as video broadcasting (and narrow-casting) increasingly looks to be the future of terrestrial telephone lines, while individuals move their personal voice communication out into the radio frequencies with cellular phones and personal, rather than locational, numbers.

---

[1] This chapter was prepared for the Scottish Council for Educational Technology 'Tactics and Trends' Conference, November 1994, and appears in the accompanying paperback, *IT: All Our Learning Futures*, forthcoming.

Bell failed to predict the use of the technology he was helping to invent; we too fail to understand (and for certain are still unable to comprehend) the magnitude and direction of future changes in the use of that technology. It is hard to remember today that the first estimate of the world market for computers considered that there might be a need for three (and people were worried their estimate might have been a bit optimistic!).

As with our technological lives, we find in our learning lives that predicting change is challenging. Education systems have been seen by politicians throughout history, and around the world, as engines for social and economic change; but, beyond the initial shock impact of education on mass literacy, substantial change is promised far more often than it is observed. There are very few areas of our lives where change has been slower than in our education systems. A series of still images from health care, travel, warfare, leisure or education would reveal, in the first four examples, dramatic and immediately apparent changes over the last seventy-five years: the size and contents of a current operating theatre, a motorway, a 'smart' missile or a charter air holiday would literally be seen as science fiction to an open-mouthed audience if we could fax the images back through time to the 1920s. But a 1990s classroom with children at individual desks, offered didactic input by a solitary teacher, working on paper from books, would seem comfortingly familiar to our 1920s observer, even if there were token changes: a computer in the corner, no slide rules, plastic surfaces, and so on.

Education has a powerful inertia which acts both to subvert change and to perpetuate itself. When in Oscar Wilde's *The Importance of Being Earnest* Jack comments that he 'knows nothing', Lady Bracknell's response is:

> I am pleased to hear it. I do not approve of anything that tampers with natural ignorance. Ignorance is like a delicate, exotic fruit; touch it, and the bloom is gone. The whole theory of modern education is radically unsound. Fortunately in England, at any rate, education produces no effect whatsoever.
> (Wilde, 1966)

Although in Scotland things may be better, the humour worked for Wilde, and still works today, because we implicitly recognize education's inertia in the face of *any* theory of modern education. It may be something of an over-generalization to suggest that at any moment in the history of education, the optimism and anticipation of those intending to engineer or predict educational change is followed by their pessimism and dismay, but it is not so far from the truth. Education is philosophically, pragmatically, demonstrably, and maybe wisely, conservative.

In the light of education's inertia and of technology's unpredictability, it is not surprising that educational computing has to date had such a small impact on the way that we manage our learning, despite significant investment; in the UK educational computing represents the single largest resource-led investment in educational change in the post-war period. Direct central investment in educational computing stands at well over £100 million (and far more in real terms), while parental and other indirect investment probably treble this amount. Inevitably with this level of investment, there has been some progress, however small, with the use of computers in the learning environment, although one can hardly describe this as a pedagogic revolution.

We can characterize the evolution of educational computing in three clear (not mutually exclusive), incremental stages.

Stage One: Topicality. Initially in the learning environment , the computer was itsel seen as the focus of attention – it was a topic in its own right. Learning outcome featured 'computer awareness'. In the UK in the early 1980s plastic injection-moulde computer keyboards (replicating the Acorn BBC B and Sinclair Spectrum) were sol through educational distributors as a tangible and slightly absurd manifestation of th view that computer keyboard familiarity was a worthwhile end in itself.

Question: What did you do at school today, Toby?
Answer: I used the computer.

'Using the computer' was a discrete and legitimate learning outcome on its own. Fo older children, computer studies as a subject was the logical extension of this 'compute as topic' phase, and a sensible use of very scarce resources. In the context of thi 'topicality' stage, the learner was seen as deficient, unfamiliar, and indeed relativel few children typically had any experience of using a computer. In terms of learnin innovation we simply see the strength of the *status quo*. The computer was quickl absorbed as 'just another topic'.

Stage Two: Surrogacy. Around the world national or regional or co-operativ ventures were providing the development of 'educational software' (Wilson, 1983) Early research had suggested that the computer offered a role as a 'neutral arbiter' i the classroom (enabling children to take risks with their learning without fear c censorship or disapproval), noted that it encouraged children to ask 'What if . . . ' questions, and observed that the computer-based learning environment was apparentl intrinsically motivating. In consequence, the computer was harnessed to deliver thos parts of the curriculum that were thought to benefit from the stimulus and interactivit offered by a computer screen. Learning outcomes included discrete knowledge acquisi tion and the development of problem-solving strategies. Computers were called upo constantly to deliver 'difficult' topics through the development of task-specific com puter programs.

Question: What did you do at school today, Melissa?
Answer: I used a computer to learn about telling the time.

This stage is characterized by a view of the computer as a surrogate teacher, embodyin a discrete and relatively small body of expertise to be trickle-fed to the 'empty vessel learner.

Computers were thus called upon to offer significantly enhanced versions of curren learning activities. But, as was commented in 1983 in a strong plea (Heppell, 1983 Wilson, 1983) for the better use of content-free software tools, in particular spread sheets, in the learning environment:

> the aims and objectives met by such computer based learning do not typically focus directly
> on the acquisition of thought processes and organisational skills necessary to exploit the
> computer as a tool in the working environment of commerce and industry.
> (Heppell, 1983)

In terms of learning, we still see the strength of the *status quo* as computers try t offer a silicon representation of the teacher's traditional role, offering discrete learnin; tasks; again, we see little innovation.

Stage Three: Progression. Exploitation of the computer as a generic tool began with the small 'useful little programs' (ULPs) that characterized early educational computing. These became dramatically outclassed by the sophisticated generic software tools that were becoming a normal part of the working world: spreadsheets, databases, word processors, desk-top publishing, modelling, communications and graphics/design. Written by teams of scores of programmers, these generic software tools outperformed and outsold education-specific software, and the cottage industry of teachers coding ULPs in their back bedrooms could not compete against heightened sophistication. The swing to generic software tools was given impetus by the need to offer progression to individual capability. Where the surrogacy stage offered discrete learning tasks, the progression stage directly addresses the issue of 'What will I do next with the capability I have developed?'

So established has this progression stage become in the UK that, with the exception of the turtle graphics and list processing of the computer language Logo, the current UK curricula can be entirely delivered with such generic, open-ended, typically content-free tools, developed for business and adopted wholesale by education for the problem-solving environment that they offered. Asking 'What if?' was never so easy:

Question: What did you do at school today, Juliette?
Answer: I tried to see if there was a link between my pulse rate and how long my arms were.
Question: How did you do that?
Answer: I used a spreadsheet.
Question: Was there a link?
Answer: No, but weight was important from our data . . .

Even this progression stage, with the curriculum 'embedding' that it engendered, is hardly yet the stuff of revolution. We have simply, but successfully, harnessed computers to offer technological awareness, problem-solving, progression and continuity.

Taking a straightforward activity like creative writing, it is easy to see the way that the innate conservatism of the education system has seemed to offer advances in the way we harness computers but has actually offered minimal real change: for more than a decade, we have enjoyed desk-top software tools capable of word processing on classroom computers. In parallel, in the workplace, the essential mutability of text in a word-processing environment, the use of machine support for grammar and spelling, the opportunities for collaborative and asynchronous endeavour and the dramatic democratizing of the publishing process by desk-top publishing have all offered the opportunity for significant changes in business practice. In schools we might expect that the way in which formative assessment is offered to a word-processed story that can be immediately redrafted ('edit this part, move this section, add a stronger introduction') would be essentially different from the way that it is offered to a handwritten one, where formative assessment focuses on how the work might be developed better next time. In practice, schools do not differentiate between the entirely different processes that computer and pen technology involve children in, nor do they teach writing in a way that reflects major changes in writing in the world of employment. Survey evidence in the UK suggests that most of children's word processing in the classroom completely ignores the process revolution that it offers to creative writers. The result is that most children are simply typing a 'best copy' of work drafted by pen elsewhere. Similarly where we might have expected the examining boards to be aware of the impact o computers on coursework development (and one major impact is to blur the lin between plagiarism and research, making the myth that we can police individua original endeavour almost impossible to sustain), there is little observable chang beyond the occasional banning of spelling checkers or an insistence on handwritte copy, which will increasingly penalize children as they evolve and hone their text processing skills. A child with word-processing skills is penalized by being forced bac into pen technology (with all its editing and redrafting problems) under externa assessment conditions. The situation is not a static one; children progress thei capability, education ignores them.

There may be good reasons for this reluctance to allow word processing to impact o the way we organize our teaching and learning: lack of staff development, lack o resources, lack of clear exemplars, failure to share models of what bad practice migh look like, hostility against the computer environment, and many more, any or all o which may be true. However, whatever the reason, we can observe that in practice th innate conservatism of the education system has limited the radical change that wor processing offers to creative writers. This is not a trivial problem; creative writers in th world outside education have almost universally harnessed computers to support then in their tasks, and we are simply not helping children develop appropriate creativ strategies to carry forward into the workplace. The same, of course, is true if we look a modelling or project planning, or any of a range of activities where computers hav changed the way we work but not the way we learn.

A defence for education's conservatism in the face of technological change might be as is observed above, that the pace and direction of change is too unpredictable to b responded to easily. Curriculum change, with the necessary consultation, piloting an refining, takes years not months, and whole technologies (cellular communications personal digital assistants, the Internet) have appeared in less time. And of course ou assessment model needs continuity to be able to preserve, with confidence, standard over any period of time. As a consequence, although we constantly debate hov children learn in general we spend little time, or research, investigating 'What do the actually learn with computer support?', 'How do we know that they've learned it?', an especially 'What might we assess?' This is not a problem confined to the UK. Aroun the world many countries are struggling with the dimensions of these problems, whil rather more countries are struggling to be aware that they are issues; none yet has an solutions.

A simple analogy is illustrative. Imagine a nation of horse riders with a clearl defined set of riding capabilities. In one short decade the motor car is invented an within that same decade many become highly competent drivers, extending th boundaries of their travel as well as developing entirely new leisure pursuits (like ca racing). At the end of the decade government ministers want to assess the true impac of automobiles on the nation's capability. Extrapolating from the present model, the would do it by putting everyone back on the horses and checking their dressage jumping and trotting as before, looking to see if the advent of cars had developed bette riders. Of course, we can all see that this would be ridiculous, yet in schools all roun Europe we are arming children with spreadsheets and assessing the same old mathem atics capabilities, we are arming them with collaborative, editable writing tools, lik word processors or desk-top publishers, and then assessing them individually as writers through a typically linear writing form that is increasingly alien to them. Where, with computers, we have even gone as far as to ban some of the powerful tools (removing spelling checkers at the point of assessment, for example), in terms of our analogy we would be taking away the car and forcing everyone back on the horse in time for the test – patently foolish.

It is not hard to imagine this cycle of technological change, accompanied by a sluggish or non-existent response from education change, continuing unchecked for some considerable time. However, there is a greater imperative for change than technological progress. As we have watched technological innovation with a detached fascination, we have failed to notice a more significant change in everyday life that will force change into education faster than we might have thought possible. As we focus on technological change, we fail to notice consequent changes that are occurring in ordinary children. It is in normal lives and in normal children that we will find the real revolution that is going to change our learning futures. These changes can be observed in adults too, but in children the changes are dramatic and significant.

What are those changes? In the Europe of the 1950s, television was unusual. It was the radio age. The generations that currently dominate our teaching professions were the children of this radio age. They retained the habit of reading too, as an important information and entertainment source. Cinema was not an everyday experience, and socially was most significant as a night out. This 'radio generation' were fed linear narrative information in a largely passive form. Families would gather round the radio and listen to favourite programmes together. TV, when it finally became available for mass consumption, needed darkened rooms, offered a tiny grey and white picture, and was again a primary narrative source. As TV developed, many houses evolved their social rooms to give the television a central focus. TVs were often built into a massive piece of furniture with all chairs facing towards it. Advertisements and programmes were dominantly narrative in form. Text was fundamentally important as a prime symbolic source of information.

However, TV in the 1990s provides an information window in a much greater information context. Children watching TV in 1995 might have a Nintendo 'Game Boy' in hand, a photo-magazine on their lap and even, inexplicably to parents, be watching while listening to their 'Walkman' headphones. Of course all this will be with the TV remote control nearby, and often with a vast number of channels on offer which are 'stepped through' at frequent intervals. Children seem to 'graze' information, and TV production companies, hoping to retain the interest of the young viewer, seek to build programmes with little narrative structure, but with complex information dimensions – text, voice-over, video-edited with great rapidity, separate background projection, music and graphics. Watch advertisements aimed at children for any number of convincing examples.

In schools there is a crisis of educational broadcasting as children find it increasingly difficult to sit for fifty minutes and offer their undivided attention to a single information source with no other choices and no video controller. Of course, it is equally uncomfortable for their teachers to sit around a radio, doing nothing else, and listen to a single aural source. We have all changed our media habits. Approaching this from a deficiency model of the learner we might claim (as many do) that children's concentration thresholds are sadly declining. However, it is equally arguable that what we are

observing are children hungry for information autonomy, adept at coping with multip
channels of information and frustratingly unstretched by monomedia.

There is considerable irony in this when one considers current developments
computer technology. Companies have struggled technically to be able to deliver t
full-screen narrative form that TV has always offered – one hour of full-screen, fu
motion video from a single disk was a multimedia 'holy grail' for so long! – and yet ju
as software and hardware manufacturers are able to deliver it, we find that learners a
beginning to' seek something else anyway. They need a browsing and active enviro
ment where learner autonomy is fundamental, where the model of informatic
represented is crucial to that browsing function, where metaphor and interface desi
are of primary importance, and where sound bites, video snatches, auditory icons a
text labels offer a complex and participatory environment that challenges the learn
and recognizes their increasing sophistication as information handlers and creator
This change is beginning to revolutionize television, but for education it is just one o
number of the changes to normal lives and normal children that will, at last, revol
tionize learning.

The computer-game culture is another significant social trend that has really on
emerged within the last decade. Almost every adult has anecdotal evidence regardi
children's high levels of capability with computer games, but again it is too easy to s
these young game players through a deficiency model of the child. Cinema in the 192
attracted comments suggesting that it would 'result in short attention spans, truan
and an explosion in juvenile crime', and the same remarks are pointed at comput
games seventy years on. Computer games are of real cultural importance to th
'information generation', and games have developed the same short fashion lives th
early cinema or pop music once had. From parents and the media today comput
games get the same sort of critical press that accompanied 'youth-orientated' film sta
like James Dean or later pop stars like the Beatles: allegedly, children can't read
socialize because they play too many computer games. They apparently becom
hopelessly addicted, social misfits trapped in an electronic never-never land. Childr
have fits, are exposed to pornography and truant from school. Or so we are led
believe. This deficiency model of children is insulting and patronizing. Worse still,
has led us to neglect the search for important and valuable learning outcomes, in t
form of new capabilities resulting from game playing. Until we are able to recogni
these emergent capabilities, we remain unable to offer progression and continuity
our children within the educational system.

Our work at UltraLab suggests that although games are imperfect, especially in t
gender stereotyping they offer, they can provide a challenging problem-solving env
onment where the players observe, question, hypothesize and test. Games can offe
vehicle for collaborative endeavour across age and gender divides. Crucially, they ha
changed the climate of expectation that surrounds children's computing experienc
Children expect delight, mental challenge and a role that is evolving from interactive
participative.

What happens when a child approaches a computer game for the first time? Taking
popular game like SEGA's Sonic the Hedgehog™ we can observe that when they beg
to play they draw on a bank of prior knowledge from playground chat and fro
previous experience. That knowledge helps them to recognize the cues and clues th
characterize the screen, but cognitively they appear to develop object prototypes

which they initially ascribe attributes or behaviours. As the game progresses they begin to internalize a taxonomy of objects and behaviour and are delighted to be challenged by good software designers who vary the behaviour of objects and cause the children to evolve sub-classes that vary the prototypical behaviour. In parallel, an understanding of the role of environment develops. For example, the child players might think, 'Here comes a round spiky thing bouncing from the right-hand side of the screen, but it's green and I'm under water so it will probably behave like this . . . ' Parents and teachers looking over children's shoulders lack the prior knowledge from playground that, fail to see the sophistication of signs and signifiers, cues and clues, lack the patience to internalize a taxonomy of prototypical behaviour, are thus unable to evolve sub-classes, and probably think the environmental cues are 'just a neat backdrop'. Inevitably, adults undervalue or fail to reward the children's achievements and are consequently unable to offer progression beyond these unacknowledged capabilities. In biology, for example, 'observe, question, hypothesize, test', together with classification, sub-classification and a careful eye to the behavioural impact of environment, is at the heart of the subject. Children, having evolved these key capabilities through gaming, are unaware that they might also be useful in the school learning context. Teachers, frustrated at the difficulty of evolving these capabilities within their biology students, might be shocked (and should be delighted) to discover that the children have evolved them anyway.

What might we conclude from all this? We constantly misjudge the pace of change. Computer technology is characterized by rapid change, but technological change typically unpredictable. Education has, perhaps wisely, been reluctant to allow technology-led change to revolutionize traditional pedagogy, and as a consequence educational computing has passed through some gentle evolutionary stages which complement existing teaching and learning practice. However, the central thesis of this chapter is that as we pass into the information age the most significant changes are occurring in the information infrastructures of that age, and especially in our ability to relate to the digital information at the heart of it. That ability is especially pronounced in children of school age. Recognizing those changes and taking advantage of them in curriculum change is an essential task for education and, for once, our formal education structures will need a swift response if opportunity is not to be wasted.

Teachers are fundamental to all this. They are learning professionals of considerable calibre. They are skilled at observing their students' capability and at developing it. They are creative and imaginative, but the curriculum must give them the space and opportunity to explore the new potential for learning that technology offers. Structures like external assessment and curriculum frameworks must allow them the freedom to continue to be good teachers in the face of changing technology and changing students. At the end of the day it will be these changing students, and the climate of expectation that they bring to their learning, that will make change happen.

It would be ironic indeed if, after resisting countless political attempts at change and after standing firm against a tide of technology, education and learning are finally changed by children. Ironic it may be, but it is also highly appropriate.

Bibliography

Academy Multimedia (1994) *Multimedia Newsletter*. Leeds: Academy Television.

Ambron, S. and Hooper, K. (eds) (1990) *Learning with Interactive Multimedia: Developing an Using Multimedia Tools in Education*. Washington: Microsoft Press.

Anglia Polytechnic University (1991) *Proposal for a Four Year Modular Primary BE [Honours]*. Brentwood: Education Department, Anglia Polytechnic University.

Baker, K. (1989) *Secretary of State for Education's Speech to the National Association of Advise in Computer Education*. London: National Association of Advisers in Computer Education

Barker, P. G. and Najah, M. (1985) Pictoral interfaces to databases. *International Journal Man-Machine Studies*, 23, pp. 423–42.

Barker, P. G. and Skipper, T. (1986) A practical introduction to authoring for computer assiste instruction. Part 7: Graphic Support for CAL. *British Journal of Educational Technology*, (3), pp. 194–212. Coventry: NCET.

Barker, J. and Tucker, R. N. (eds) (1990) *The Interactive Learning Revolution: Multimedia Education and Training*. London: Kogan Page.

Barker, P. (ed.) (1989) *Multi-media Computer Assisted Learning*. London: Kogan Page.

Barnett, C. (1981) Computer vision can show us what the mind can imagine. *Smithsonie Magazine*, 12 (3), pp. 106–13.

Bernstein, B. (1990) *The Structure of Pedagogic Discourse*. London: Routledge.

Bruner, J.S. (1982) *Toward a Theory of Instruction*. Cambridge, Mass.: Harvard Universi Press.

Cambell, R. and Hanlon, P. (1990) HyperCard: A New Deal in the Classroom. In Ambron an Hooper (1990), pp. 258–86.

Cockroft, W. H. (1982) *Mathematics Counts: Report of the Committee Enquiring Into t Teaching of Mathematics in Schools*. London: HMSO.

Collins, J. G. and Lengel, S. (1990) HyperCard in education: Perspectives from the field. Ambron and Hooper (1990), pp. 189–98.

DES (1988a) *The Education Reform Act*. London: HMSO.

DES (1988b) *English for Ages Five to Eleven*. London: HMSO.

DES (1988c) *Mathematics for Ages Five to Sixteen*. London: HMSO.

DES (1988d) *Science for Ages Five to Sixteen*. London: HMSO.

DES (1989a) *Circular 5/89*. London: HMSO.

DES (1989b) *Circular 16/89*. London: HMSO.

DES (1989c) *Curriculum Matters 15: Information Technology from Five to Sixteen*. Londo HMSO.

DES (1989d) *Technology from Five to Sixteen*. London: HMSO.

DES (1990a) *Examination Entries for Computer Studies from 1984 to 1987*. London: HMSO.

DES (1990b) *Technology in the National Curriculum*. London: HMSO.

DES (1991a) *Geography in the National Curriculum*. London: HMSO.

DES (1991b) *History in the National Curriculum*. London: HMSO.

DES (1991c) *Modern Foreign Languages in the National Curriculum*. London: HMSO.

DES (1992a) *Art in the National Curriculum*. London: HMSO.

DES (1992b) *Music in the National Curriculum*. London: HMSO.

DES (1992c) *Physical Education in the National Curriculum*. London: HMSO.

Evans, N. (1994) Article. *Education Guardian* 24 May.

Fields, J. (1990) *The Challenge Ahead: Information Technology in the Primary School Curriculum*. Nafferton, North Humberside: Studies in Education.

Geoffrion, L. D. and Geoffrion, O. P. (1983) *Computers and Reading Instruction*. Reading, Mass.: Addison-Wesley Publishing Company.

Glyn-Jones, F. (1994) Multimedia in schools. In *The Head's Legal Guide*. Kingston upon Thames: Croner Publications Ltd.

Goodman, D. (1990) *The Complete Hypercard 2.0 Handbook*. New York: Bantam Books.

Habermas, J. (1971) *Towards a Rational Society*. London: Heinemann.

Haddow, Sir W. H. (1931) *Reports on the Consultative Committee on the Primary School*. London: Board of Education.

Hart, B. (1990) We can't afford the National Curriculum in primary schools. Unpublished Paper. Sheffield: City of Sheffield Local Education Authority.

Haywood, J. (1969) I Never Thought I'd Live to Be a Hundred. On *To Our Children's Children's Children*, Moody Blues. London: Decca Record Company.

Heppell, C. and Millwood, R. (1992) *Work Rooms: User Guide*. Brentwood, Essex: The UltraLab, Anglia Polytechnic University.

Heppell, S. (1983) The use of business software as a content free teaching tool: Emulation or assimilation?. In Kibby and Hartley (1983).

Heppell, S. (1990) Multimedia in the primary learning environment: The challenge ahead. In Fields (1990).

Heppell, S. *et al.* (1991a) Broken calculator. In *Work Rooms*. Computer Software. England: Anglia Polytechnic University.

Heppell, S. *et al.* (1991b) *Work Rooms*. Computer Software. Brentwood, Essex: Anglia Polytechnic University.

Heppell, S. (1993) Children, games and gains, *Times Educational Supplement Computer Update*. London: Times Educational Supplement.

HMI (1987) *Curriculum Matters 3: Mathematics from 5 to 16*. London: HMSO.

HMI (1991) *Survey of 700 Lessons Observed with an Information Technology Component*. London: HMSO.

HMI (1992) *Annual Report on Education in England 1990–1991*. London: HMSO.

Hofmeister, J. F. (1990). The birth of HyperSchool. In Ambron and Hooper (1990), pp. 200–21.

Hoyles, C. (1988) *Girls and Computers: General Issues and Case Studies of Logo in the Mathematics Classroom*. London: Institute of Education, London University.

Hunter, P. (1992) *Pendown*. Computer Software. Cambridge: Longman Logotron.

Jek, K. J. programmer. Frank Voon, original idea (1990) *Vincent: 1853 to 1890*. Computer Software.

Jenkins, Y. (1990) Multimedia technology: Tools for early learning. In Ambron and Hooper, pp. 112–23.

Kennedy, M. and Robinson, G. (1991) *The Art of Design*. Brentwood, Essex: Anglia Polytechnic University.

Kibby, M. R. and Hartley, J. R. (eds) (1983) *CAL 83: Computer Assisted Learning Symposium*. Oxford: Pergamon Press.

Lodge, J. (1969) Eyes of a child. On *To Our Children's Children's Children*, Moody Blues. London: Decca Record Company.

Logotron (1990) *Logo*. Computer Software. Cambridge: Longman Logotron.

McMahon, H. *et al.* (1990) *Computers in the Third World: Examples, Experiences, and Issues*. London: Macmillan.

McNally, D. W. (1974) *Piaget, Education and Teaching*. Lewes, Sussex: New Educational Press.
MEP (1984) *Primary Maths and Micros*. London: MEP Primary Project.
MEP (1985a) *Infant and First Schools: The Role of the Micro*. London: MEP Primary Project.
MEP (1985b) *Language Development in the Primary School: The Role of the Microcomputer*. London: MEP Primary Project.
MEP (1985c) *Posing and Solving Problems Using Control Technology: A Teacher Training Pack*. London: MEP Primary Project.
MEP (1985d) *Posing and Solving Problems With a Micro*. London: MEP Primary Project.
Miller, L. and Olson, J. (1994) Putting the computer in its place: A study of teaching with technology. *Journal of Curriculum Studies* **26** (March–April).
Mintz, D. (1990) Launching teachers into a HyperWorld. In Ambron and Hooper (1990), pp. 155–88.
Multimedia Laboratory (1990) *The Encyclopaedia of Multimedia*. San Francisco: Apple Computer Inc.
NCC (1990a) *Curriculum Guidance 8: Education for Citizenship*. London: HMSO.
NCC (1990b) *Guidance Document on the Whole Curriculum*. London: HMSO.
NUT (1992) *Curriculum Guidelines*. London: NUT.
Neurath, O. (1939) *Modern Man in the Making*. New York: Knopf.
Neurath, O. (1980) *International Picture Language* (A Facsimile Reprint of the 1936 Edition). Reading: Department of Typography and Graphic Communication, University of Reading.
Nicol, A. (1990) Children using HyperCard. In Ambron and Hooper (1990), pp. 141–54.
Nisbet, R. A. (1970) *The Sociological Tradition*. London: Heinemann.
OFSTED (1993) *Handbook for the Inspection of Schools*. London: HMSO.
Paivio, A. (1980) Imagery as a private audio-visual aid. *Instructional Science*, 9. Dordrecht, Netherlands: Kluwer Academic Publishers, pp. 295–309.
Papert, S. (1982) *Mindstorms: Children, Computers, and Powerful Ideas*. Brighton, Sussex: Harvester Press.
Parry, M. T. (1985) Trying times with a Turtle. *Journal of Computer Assisted Learning*, **1** (2).
Riley, D. *et al.* (1990) *Design for Active Learning*. London: Centre for Educational Studies, King's College, London University.
SCAA (1994) *Information Technology in the National Curriculum*. Draft Proposals. London: HMSO.
Sempor, R. (1990) HyperCard and Education: Reflections on the Hyper boom. In Ambron and Hooper (1990), pp. 52–67.
Singh, P. (1993) Institutional discourse and practice: A case study of the social construction of technological competence in the primary classroom. *British Journal of Sociology of Education*, **14** (1).
Stebbins, B. (1990) Using HyperCard in Apple classrooms of tomorrow. In Ambron and Hooper (1990), pp. 224–55.
Tediman Software (1988) *Folio*. Computer Software. Wisbech, Cambridgeshire: ESM.
Waern, Y. and Rollenhagen, C. (1983) Reading text from Visual Display Units (VDUs). *International Journal of Man-Machine Studies* **18**.
Wilde, O. (1966) *The Importance of Being Earnest*. London: Eyre Methuen.
Williams, P. and Jinks, D. (1985) *Design and Technology 5–12*. Lewes: Falmer Press.
Wilson, N. (1983) Educational software development and exchange: Present and future. In Kibby and Hartley (1983).
Winter, R. (1987) *Action Research and the Nature of Social Enquiry*. Aldershot: Avebury, Gower Publishing Company Ltd.

Computer Software

BBC (1986) *The Doomsday Interactive Video Discs*. London: BBC Enterprises Ltd.

Brown, M. (1992) *Arthur's Teacher Trouble*. Novata, Calif.: Broderbund Software Inc.

Grimm, L., Caswell, D. and Kirkpatrick, L. (1991) *The Playroom*. Novata, Calif.: Broderbund Software Inc.

Gustaffson, R. and Young, A. (1992) *Kid Pix*. Novata, Calif.: Broderbund Software Inc.

Hickman, C. (1992) *Kid Pix*. Novata, Calif.: Broderbund Software Inc.

Mayer, M. (1992) *Just Grandma and Me*. Novata, Calif.: Broderbund Software Inc.

UltraLab (1994a) *Le Carnaval des Animaux*. CD-ROM Disc. Brentwood, Essex: UltraLab, Anglia Polytechnic University.

UltraLab (1994b) *Insights for Teachers and Parents*. CD-ROM Disc. Brentwood, Essex: UltraLab, Anglia Polytechnic University.

Name Index

Subject Index